a little bit of

mindfulness

a little bit of
mindfulness

an introduction
to being present

AMY LEIGH MERCREE

STERLING ETHOS
New York

STERLING ETHOS
New York

STERLING ETHOS and the distinctive Sterling Ethos logo
are registered trademarks of Sterling Publishing Co., Inc.

Text © 2018 Amy Leigh Mercree

ISBN 978-1-4549-3224-6
ISBN 978-1-4549-3249-9 (e-book)

For information about custom editions, special sales, and premium
purchases, please contact specialsales@unionsquareandco.com.

Printed in India

6 8 10 12 14 13 11 9 7 5

unionsquareandco.com

Cover and interior design by Melissa Farris
Cover and interior illustration by Marish/Shutterstock.com

This book is dedicated to the
goddesses of the light who guide me and
challenge me to live a mindful life.

contents

INTRODUCTION

Mindfulness has become a popular buzzword in the last several years. But it's so much more than a trendy hashtag. It's an opportunity to deepen your experience of reality and live a life of meaning and fulfillment.

The concept of mindfulness is all about being present, fully in the moment, and becoming aware of yourself and your surroundings. It also means practicing non-reactivity; that is, not becoming overwhelmed by your environment. Celebrities, scientists, athletes, and people from all walks of life tout the amazing physical and mental benefits of mindfulness; and scientific research backs up many of their experiences. Incredibly, studies have shown that daily mindfulness practices can reduce cortisol, the stress hormone in our bodies, by more than 50 percent.

The practice of mindfulness exists in many cultures, but the North American practice of mindfulness was popularized by Jon Kabat-Zinn in the 1960s. While traveling in Asia, he became a master practitioner of mindfulness and meditation. He brought his experiences back to the United States and created Mindfulness-Based Stress Reduction (MBSR) which remains popular to this day.

Mindfulness isn't just for the rich and famous—people all over the world have taken it up in an effort to understand themselves and function better in modern life. Each and every one of us can learn something from the centuries-old meditative practice. If you are among the many who are searching for a way to increase your quality of life, look no farther.

1
what is mindfulness?

A mindful life can be an open doorway to greater peace and tranquility. Practicing mindfulness doesn't have to be a complete overhaul of your lifestyle. It's easy to fit in a moment here or there to stop and take in your surroundings, which is an essential factor in the quest to become more mindful. Simple daily activities can be perfect starting points for incorporating elements of mindfulness into your life.

One way to prioritize mindful living is to pay attention to your breath. This practice is a basic one and can be performed anywhere at any time of day. For beginners, it's important to be aware of your breath as a starting point for more complex mindfulness practices, including meditation. Even advanced practitioners of mindfulness can refocus and become in tune with their bodies and minds through breath practice. To begin, close your eyes if possible, and breath in gently through your nose. Make sure you can feel the breath all the way into your lungs. Straighten your core and lift your chin to guarantee a deep breath. When you're ready, exhale slowly through your mouth and relax your body. Repeat until your breaths are consistent and your focus is centered on the in-and-out motion. We will practice this technique step by step later in this book.

Another well-loved technique is to try to walk mindfully. Whether you are going on a walk specifically to relax and center yourself or you're headed to your next destination by foot, mindful walking can improve your day. Pay attention to the way your body moves as you walk and the frequency of your breaths. Concentrate on your feet connecting with the earth as you walk. Focus within, and then slowly reincorporate the sights and sounds of the world around you. Once you master the art of walking mindfully, even mundane travel will be a chance for you to refresh your brain.

Even everyday activities like eating can be an opportunities for mindfulness. In our fast-paced life, we may sometimes find ourselves racing through meals. Breakfasts are rushed, lunch is just a quick break at work, and even an evening meal with loved ones is often finished all too soon. Eating mindfully, on the other hand, has both spiritual and physical benefits. One important aspect of eating mindfully is ensuring that each bite is thoroughly chewed. Savoring the flavor, texture, and smell of your meal will allow you to enjoy it and slow down. Eating with others offers the opportunity to talk and connect while nourishing your body.

A mindful moment can be as simple as taking time to pause. Even brief, momentary check-ins with yourself will allow you to experience the benefits of mindfulness. Take a minute in between chores, destinations, and travel to observe the world around you and reflect on what's going on in your own mind. We can get so caught up in checking activities off a list that our days become filled with routine actions. Something as simple as setting your phone down before responding to a message or stopping for a moment before answering the door can make a huge difference in your awareness. Mini pauses help re-center us throughout the day.

A natural result of mindfulness is self-reflection. Take time throughout your day to notice your thoughts and feelings about the world around you. Sometimes we can stress about our emotions and confuse them with our deepest selves—we are not our thoughts, and it's possible to separate ourselves from them and observe them without judgment. Don't let your mind go down a long path because of a single troubling thought. It's easy to become depressed or anxious when we feel isolated. Being mindful and practicing self-reflection is a simple but effective way to stop allowing ourselves to get carried away in our negative thoughts.

When we can fully ground ourselves through mindfulness, we can open the door to let others into our lives. To build real connections, we have to allow ourselves to let go of our judgment, preconceived notions, and need to respond. When these things are removed, we can completely open ourselves to others and fully listen to what they are saying. You may be amazed at how much your relationships change for the better when you start practicing mindfulness. To multiply the effect, recruit others to join you in your newfound practice.

Mindful meditation can be a shared activity and may strengthen the bonds between family, friends, and partners.

Use your senses—smell, taste, touch, sight, and hearing—to fully soak in the world around you. Being mindful allows you to focus on your own thoughts, feelings, and actions, and it also helps you better understand and accept your surroundings. Starting within your own body and working outward, notice what is happening: in what position are you holding your body? Is it a comfortable or uncomfortable one? How does your clothing feel against your skin? What's happening in the room around you? Are there any smells or sounds? How about the world outside? Can you hear or see anything going on? Answer each question to yourself and accept it without judgment or emotion. The simple act of observing and redirecting thoughts is a kind of mini-meditation on its own. This is being mindful. It is that simple!

Mindfulness and meditation can allow you to fully relax and take time for much-needed rest. Jerry Seinfeld credits meditation for his sanity during nine years of intensive work on his network show. He said, "While everybody was having lunch I would do Transcendental Meditation. That was how I survived the nine years. Those 20 minutes in the middle of the day saved me."

Mindfulness can help clear away negative energy and create a space for creativity and ingenuity. Steve Jobs talked about it by saying the mind was incredibly restless. He said, "If you try to calm it, it only makes things worse, but over time it does calm, and when it does, there's room to hear more subtle things—that's when your intuition starts to blossom and you start to see things more clearly and be in the present more."

Meditation can also be an outlet to escape from social roles and daily life stressors. Soledad O'Brien has talked about meditation and the resulting mindfulness in the following way: "[Meditation] allows me to experience a state of deep rest and relaxation that can be game-changing; and sometimes a life saver in a crazy world. . . . It helps alleviate stress and pressure when you're trying to balance life and being a mother."

2

the history
of mindfulness

The popularity of mindfulness can be traced to ancient spiritual practices. What we now call mindfulness has developed from traditions across the world dating back thousands of years. Mindfulness draws on religions and practices with roots in the Eastern world and especially in Eastern religions. Today's hot yoga groups, Mindfulness-Based Stress Reduction (MBSR) classes, and online meditation videos are offshoots of rituals steeped in history.

HINDUISM

Hinduism, widely known as the oldest religion in the world, came about as a mix of many smaller religious traditions in the East, mostly around what would now be considered India. Because of Hinduism's complex history, there is no single credited founder or distinct creation date. It is made up of ancient Vedic traditions that were the practices of a group of people during the Vedic period (around 1500–600 BCE) in what is now northern India. During the 1800s, writers in Great Britain began lumping Vedic practices together and referring to them as Hinduism, and the modern interpretation of Hinduism in the West was born.

Present-day Hindu concepts include the worship of many gods, temple traditions, and dharma (a principle of cosmic order and a prescription for the right way to live life). The *Bhagavad Gita*, a sacred text in the Hindu tradition, makes mention of Vedic meditation and yoga—both of which have come to be intertwined with the concept of mindfulness. Practitioners and others interested in the history of mindfulness can consider Hinduism one of the foundational building blocks of the movement.

BUDDHISM

Buddhism, another crucial element to understanding the history of mindfulness, has a much more concrete history. Founded around 400 BCE by the man who came to be known as the Buddha (originally known as Siddhartha Gautama) in what is now India and Nepal, Buddhism was inspired by many elements of the Hindu tradition. Both evolved in the East, both believe in a natural cosmic order, and both incorporate elements that became the basis for modern mindfulness practice.

The main focus of Buddhism is to lead followers on the path to enlightenment. The first step on the journey of enlightenment is *sati*, which translates to mindfulness. The term *sati* in its original Sanskrit translation means to remember or to bear in mind. It implies an awareness of how things relate to other things—in other words, any idea or feeling that mindfulness practitioners have is just one thought in a sea of other thoughts. A core idea of mindfulness practice is hearing, accepting, and moving past our thoughts. In this way, *sati* is the foundation of mindfulness and nonjudgmental acceptance.

Because of how crucial mindfulness is as a Buddhist concept, many Western mindfulness practitioners have studied under Buddhist experts. Modern mindfulness exercises in the West owe much to Buddhism and Buddhist leaders as their influence has helped shape what we now consider to be mindfulness practice.

MINDFULNESS AND YOGA

The history of yoga is complex, and the word *yoga* itself has taken on many different meanings over thousands of years. Our idea of modern Western yoga does not necessarily line up with its more obscure origins. However, it's helpful to try to understand the beginnings of yoga to reveal more about modern mindfulness practice.

Around 3300 BCE, the term *yoga* first appeared in the Vedic scripts from early Hinduism. Vedic priests were noted to perform sacrifices (*yajna*), and some researchers believe that the poses in which they sacrificed things were early forms of yoga. In the third century, the word *yoga* began appearing more frequently in reference to a spiritual and meditative practice known as Yogachara. It had eight steps of meditation and was the first thoroughly explained practice that links yoga to modern mindfulness.

Later, in the fifth century, yoga truly became a core component of many religious practices, including those of Hinduism, Jainism, and Buddhism. It was a spiritual practice much more than a physical one and was unlike modern yoga used for exercise. The spirituality of yoga blended together some basic values: one was reflecting on one's mental state and using mindful yoga to understand it. The goal was to transcend physical and mental suffering to reach a different level of being (which references the concept of enlightenment in Hinduism and Buddhism). Another value was to broaden the consciousness of yoga practitioners. Yoga was a path to mystical transcendence, and from there, it was seen as a way to ultimately enter another body or transcend the current one.

In this same era, yoga became stratified by yogi practice and yoga practice. The former refers to the more supernatural elements of mindfulness and the ability of yogis to expand their consciousness in order to transcend their earthly bodies. Meanwhile, yoga practice became focused on training the mind and practicing meditation, which is where the modern concept of mindfulness evolved from.

YOGA'S TRANSITION TO THE WESTERN WORLD

In the 1890s, yoga first came to the attention of the Western world. Some of yoga's popularity is due to the work of Swami Vivekananda, a Hindu monk who toured Europe and the United States in the late nineteenth century promoting knowledge of Hinduism. Vivekananda showcased the yoga sutras to the West as well. These sutras were writings from 400 CE that detail yoga traditions such as removing excessive thoughts from one's mind and focusing on a single thought.

Later, in the twentieth century, Hatha yoga (what is most practiced in the United States today) gained popularity. In the 1930s it first came to light, and its popularity peaked in the 1960s, when the youth revolution and hippie lifestyle took over the U.S. With this revolution came an introduction of Eastern concepts, most notably mindfulness and yoga. After the 1960s, the physical and health benefits of yoga were popularized, and it became a practice not just for mental relaxation (mindfulness) but also for exercise. Yoga continues to be popular in the U.S., and many modern gyms offer classes. However, the mindfulness building blocks of yoga are sometimes less emphasized in many of today's practices.

The arrival of mindfulness in the U.S. is mostly due to the work of Jon Kabat-Zinn. Dr. Kabat-Zinn is a professor at the University of Massachusetts Medical School. Before he was in academia, Kabat-Zinn was introduced to Buddhism when he was studying at the Massachusetts Institute of Technology (MIT). A Zen missionary named Philip Kapleau came to speak at MIT and inspired Kabat-Zinn as a young student. Afterward, Kabat-Zinn began studying meditation and Buddhist teachings at the Insight Meditation Society. Eventually he became a teacher at the Society, and in 1979, he founded his own institution: the Stress Reduction Clinic at the University of Massachusetts Medical School.

This shift from Buddhist-centric concepts to independent "stress relief" classes represents the divergent paths of mindfulness in the United States. One path embraces the spiritual and supernatural foundation of mindfulness, and another (popularized by Kabat-Zinn) has become a standalone practice that is independent of religion. Kabat-Zinn's stress relief classes became formalized into his creation, Mindfulness-Based Stress Reduction (MBSR). MBSR is an eight-week course that is structured on mindfulness practices and taught by certified teachers all over the U.S. By removing some of the religious elements, Kabat-Zinn was able to reach people of all backgrounds and religions. Although mindfulness has its roots in Buddhist and Hindu origins, modern practices have become mainly focused on mental and physical health instead of spirituality.

As evidenced by the broad acceptance of Kabat-Zinn's MBSR techniques, the mental benefits of mindfulness cannot be overstated. Many schools of psychology have taken note of this popularity and incorporated mindful practices as an element of mental healing.

MINDFULNESS-BASED COGNITIVE THERAPY (MBCT)

Inspired by Mindfulness-Based Stress Reduction, MBCT is a program specifically intended to target clinical depression (also known as major depressive disorder) and is helpful for people with physical trauma and brain injury. MBCT integrates science with mindfulness to help patients suffering from mental disorders. It is a modified version of cognitive therapy that incorporates meditation and breathing exercises. MBCT therapists are specially trained to help break patterns of negative thought. MBCT is a type of group therapy that meets once a week for a two-hour session. Therapists act as group leaders and help patients learn meditative techniques during their sessions.

Research has shown MBCT is effective in treating major depressive disorder and can help decrease the frequency and strength of depressive episodes in people with major physical trauma like traumatic brain injuries or certain vascular diseases.

POSITIVE PSYCHOLOGY

While MBCT and MBSR have become popular for their effects on depressed patients, the field of positive psychology has widely embraced mindfulness meditation as a tool for anyone, regardless of diagnosis, to improve mental health. The benefit of mindful practices is that they can be applied in a wide range of situations, with varying levels of involvement. For positive psychology therapists, the philosophy of mindfulness that Eastern religion and culture started is now an applicable, proven method for helping people across the world.

A 2016 study researched the integration of mindful practices with positive psychology in a program called the Positive Mindful Program. This experiment used mindfulness training to supplement classic positive psychology interventions in an attempt to increase participant well-being. The result was a booming success and showed that mindfulness and positive psychology go hand in hand.

MODERN MINDFULNESS MOVEMENTS

Jon Kabat-Zinn defines *mindfulness* as "the psychological process of bringing one's attention to the internal and external experiences occurring in the present moment, which can be developed through the practice of meditation and other training." By using this definition, it's clear to see that the applicability of mindfulness stretches across generations and into every facet of modern life. Living a mindful life is, at its core, a daily practice to notice and savor each moment. Heightened awareness of physical sensations, the surrounding environment, thoughts, and feelings is the starting point for mindful living. Accepting these things as they are (not "right" or "wrong") is the key component to exemplifying mindfulness.

In the twenty-first century, mindfulness has reached many parts of the Western world, from education to business to government, making clear the dramatic benefits to well-being that mindfulness can bring about.

SCHOOLS AND EDUCATION

University research has shown a correlation between mindfulness and attention, and these findings have been used to support programs for grade schoolers across the U.S. Schools in Miami (Mindful Kids Miami, Inc.), Los Angeles (The Inner Kids Program), Baltimore (The Holistic Life Foundation), and Richmond (Mindful Life Project) have all implemented programs aimed at teaching educators how to include mindfulness techniques into the classroom, as well as directly teaching children how to self-regulate using mindful actions. Additionally, the MindUP program trains teachers across the U.S. (more than 1,000 schools) about mindfulness.

LAW

Many law firms now offer classes in mindfulness, and Harvard Law School's prestigious Program on Negotiation has hosted mindfulness workshops.

BUSINESS

Several large corporations have begun investing in mindfulness programs to help their company culture. Google, Apple, Procter & Gamble, General Mills, Mayo Clinic, and the U.S. Army are just some of the companies that have implemented mindful techniques, including meditation breaks and mindfulness coaching.

GOVERNMENT

Mindfulness training has entered many government organizations' continuing education curricula. In the Western world, both the U.S. and the U.K. have implemented government-sponsored mindfulness programs: Coping Strategies for U.S. Armed Forces personnel, and a mindfulness session led by Ruby Wax, a prominent UK actress and author of a book on mindfulness, for the members of the British Parliament.

3

the science
of mindfulness

What do you associate with the word *mindfulness*? An idyllic, tropical beach? A person sitting calmly? A sunset? A combination of all three? Mindfulness can indeed look like this, but our preconceived notions of it rarely capture the whole picture. It can be practiced in many forms. And most importantly, it is accessible and available to anyone interested in utilizing the techniques. As science begins to explore the effects of mindfulness on the mind and body, we can better understand the benefits of the practice. We are also able to start expanding our concept of mindfulness to encompass much more than the calm scene on the beach and, instead, allow it into the business of our own lives.

Mindfulness means intentionally being aware and engaged in the present moment. It involves awareness of your own mind and your present environment in a nonjudgmental way. Mindfulness can be inserted into any activity, ranging from a mindful walk to a mindful chat over coffee with a close friend. There is no one correct path to mindfulness. While most research focuses on mindfulness meditation, other techniques, such as yoga and tai chi, are also associated with it. Mindfulness techniques can be applied to multiple settings and situations and are reported by many to enhance well-being.

WHO STUDIES MINDFULNESS? A FEW OF THE TOP SCIENTISTS AND INSTITUTES

Psychologists, medical doctors, and neuroscientists are just a few of the professionals who are focusing their studies to explore mindfulness. Research on mindfulness has gained attention since the early 2000s and continues to be of interest to both scientists and the general public.

The University of Massachusetts Center for Mindfulness

One of the most prolific mindfulness researchers is Dr. Jon Kabat-Zinn, a professor of medicine at Harvard University and founder of the University Massachusetts Center for Mindfulness. Kabat-Zinn created a stress-reduction program called Mindfulness-Based Stress Reduction (MBSR). The program is specifically geared toward people with pain or health issues difficult to treat in a Western medical setting. Kabat-Zinn published his first book outlining the MBSR technique, *Full Catastrophe Living*, in 1990. Since then he has published many scientific studies that explore the effect mindfulness has on the mind and body. The UMass Center for Mindfulness is a significant hub for mindfulness research and explores the effects of mindfulness on the brain, on behavior, and as a mode of treatment. Currently, Dr. Judson Brewer, an associate professor and research director, oversees the research at the center. His research focus includes mindfulness as a treatment for addiction, specifically cigarette smoking and food cravings, as well as neuroimaging tools to explore how mindfulness affects the brain.

The Jha Lab at the University of Miami

Dr. Amishi Jha, PhD, is a neuroscientist and mindfulness researcher based at the University of Miami. She is the founder and director of The Jha Lab, where she and her team explore the effect of mindfulness on processing emotions, attention, memory, and focus. The lab also focuses on the effect mindfulness has on members of the military and how different mindfulness practices can be beneficial in the short and long term.

The Center for Mindfulness and Human Potential at the University of California

Dr. Michael Mrazek is the research director at the Center for Mindfulness and Human Potential at the University of California, Santa Barbara. Like other centers researching mindfulness, here some of the popular topics of study are the brain, attention, and memory. Mrazek also focuses on the effect mindfulness has on students, especially on their performance on standardized tests.

The Mindful Awareness Research Center at the University of California, Los Angeles

Dr. Dan Siegel is a clinical professor of psychology at the University of California, Los Angeles, and founding codirector of the Mindful Awareness Research Center. In addition to offering mindfulness courses, retreats, and events, the Mindful Awareness Research Center is also a leader in mindfulness research. Siegel now runs Mindsight Institute, an online site that offers courses and retreats to explore mindfulness and its effects on the brain.

WHAT MINDFULNESS SCIENCE SAYS

Many practitioners of mindfulness report that it is a valuable and effective technique, and scientific studies are helping to shed light on why mindfulness is beneficial to so many people. Reports offer promising evidence that mindfulness is a healthy and accessible technique for the mind and the body.

Reduces Rumination

Reflecting on different topics can be helpful and can lead to new ideas and realizations. However, sometimes this reflection runs in a circle, trapping you in a whirl of never-ending and often unproductive thoughts. This can lead to rumination, or the tendency to get stuck on past ideas or memories, and can be an obstacle in moving forward or finding personal growth.

In one study, a group of people attended a ten-day mindfulness meditation retreat. After the retreat, the group showed better memory and ability to pay attention to tasks and reported less rumination and depressive symptoms when compared to a non-mindful control group. The test group also reported feeling mindful and had increased attention and focus when compared to the control group.

Mindfulness for Stress

We live in a fast-paced world that often leads to overscheduling, multitasking, and stressing out. Many studies have linked mindfulness to stress reduction and improved mental health, indicating that it may be a treatment option for medical professionals to offer patients. One report compiled thirty-nine different studies on the effect of mindfulness-based therapy for multiple conditions, including anxiety and depression. Patients were compared before and after treatment and reported any improvement in anxiety and mood disorders. The positive results suggest that mindfulness-based therapy techniques can help treat anxiety and mood-disorders.

Managing Emotions

Mindfulness doesn't ease your emotions, but there is evidence that it helps you control them. When strong emotions arise, they can be overwhelming at times, hanging like a dark cloud over daily tasks. Mindfulness techniques can help regulate these emotions and may equip practitioners with the ability to better handle and recover from emotionally challenging times. One research study explored the relationship between mindfulness training and emotional expression. Participants were divided into two groups: one received mindfulness training, and one did not. The participants in the mindfulness-training group took a course for eight weeks that met for two-hour sessions and showcased many kinds of mindfulness, including yoga, walking, and seated meditation. The group was also given after-session homework to emphasize training from class that included guided meditations and activities to enhance awareness. A primary teaching point in the course was to be aware of difficult circumstances and emotions but to separate the self from the experience. After the eight-week training was complete, participants were shown brief clips of movies to provoke sadness and were then asked to rate their level of sadness on a five-point scale. Results showed that the mindfulness-training group reported lower levels of depression, anxiety, and bodily discomfort when compared to the control group. Another study explored the effect of mindfulness meditation on the ability to recover from emotionally triggering photos. The participants had a wide range of mindfulness experience, ranging from the totally new (one month) to the experienced (twenty-nine years). Participants familiar with mindfulness meditation were more capable of focusing on a cognitive task after being presented with an emotion-evoking photo. This suggests that mindfulness meditation can help you control your emotions, including how they influence your task performance and your ability to function when faced with emotionally triggering material and events.

Mindfulness and the Immune System

The beneficial effects that mindfulness has on your mental health translate to physical health as well. Symptoms of anxiety and depression are known to lower the effectiveness of your immune system. Mindfulness helps control emotions and improves these symptoms. A 2016 study investigated the relationship between mindfulness meditation and five variables: inflammatory proteins in the body, gene expression, immune cell count, immune cell antiaging, and antibody response. The researchers analyzed twenty different studies, totaling more than 1,600 participants. They found that mindfulness meditation correlates with reduced inflammation, increased immune cell antiaging, and increased antibodies. This research provides preliminary evidence of the positive effect mindfulness meditation has on the body.

Mindfulness May Help Improve Relationships

Family, friendships, and community are all important to mental well-being, as they provide a sense of belonging and support. Scientific studies are exploring not only the benefits of mindfulness on mental and physical levels but also the effects it has on social relationships. Research suggests that the ability to handle emotional stress along with the ability to communicate emotions and be empathetic are major components in healthy social relationships. A 2014 study focused on the effect mindfulness meditation had on the ability of people to interpret the emotions of others. Participants were given a five-minute course in mindfulness meditation and then were asked to complete specific tasks designed to measure empathy. Results showed that mindfulness meditation participants showed higher levels of empathetic understanding, a quality that can help communication and understanding in any relationship.

Mindfulness not only helps you empathize more, but also there is evidence that it makes you feel more satisfied in your relationships. One study examined the impact that mindfulness training had on married couples. The study found that mindfulness was associated with better communication and an ability to deal with strong emotions, such as anger, in a relationship. Unsurprisingly, married couples with the ability to communicate difficult emotions more easily reported higher satisfaction within their marriage. Researchers suggest that mindfulness helps people be aware of their thoughts and their effect on others and allows them to discuss issues more openly. This shows that mindfulness techniques can be used in various social situations and can help improve relationships.

Improve Working Memory and Focus

In a world of multitasking, finding your focus is key to being productive and feeling grounded. Because mindfulness is centered on staying aware in the present, your ability to control your focus improves. Working memory is also a major player; it is the one part of short-term memory that relates to how efficiently you process subconscious information, such as speaking and understanding. A study from the Jha Lab explored the effect of mindfulness meditation on a military group before deployment. One part of the group participated in an eight-week mindfulness training while the rest did not. Results showed that the mindfulness meditation group had better working-memory than the non-meditating group.

Another study explored how mindfulness affects focus. The mindfulness training group scored higher on attention and focus than the group without mindfulness training.

The science of mindfulness is still in its infancy, but many people are using mindfulness techniques to improve well-being. The support of various institutes exploring mindfulness will surely create more data that will help us better understand this beneficial technique and how it relates to well-being.

4

quieting the
chemical symphony

Within your body at any given time is an elaborate and finely tuned orchestra of chemical messages being shared throughout every system and synapse you have. The violin section is harmoniously releasing insulin to tell your body how to receive the sweetness of life. The trumpet section is boldly sharing testosterone to tell your body how to help you live your passion. The flute section is dancing among the flowers, issuing forth estrogen to make your hair soft and your skin supple. The harp section intones the uplifting hormone serotonin to regulate your mood. The cello section provides the resonant sound of thyroxin as it modulates your metabolism. The piano section fills in the melody to enliven your days with dopamine as it allows you to experience pleasure and perceive your world with accuracy.

This incredible chemical symphony has evolved to direct and optimize the function of our bodies. When you think about it, it's pretty amazing that these tiny molecules are the directors of our experience of reality. Our feelings are hormonally influenced. Our physical experience of life is a result of our hormones. When we feel hungry it's leptin and ghrerlin.

But, there's something in modern life that tends to throw a wrench in the works of our harmonious chemical symphony: stress. With too much stress, our cortisol can disregulate. And from there many things can be affected. Lucky for us, we have a clinically proven, completely natural, drug-free remedy to combat stress at our fingertips at any given moment. Mindfulness.

Mindfulness has been used since ancient times to regulate the mind and body. An important aspect of mindfulness practice is the awareness of your breath—learning to pay attention to your breath and to the quality of it. Mindfulness refers to the practice of bringing your awareness to the present moment consciously and intentionally. This practice fosters the ability to self-regulate thoughts and emotions by bringing your attention to yourself and approaching yourself from an observer mentality. By noticing physical sensations and mental processes nonjudgmentally and without attachment, you can become an external observer. Through this role, you can learn more about yourself and your true nature. Practices and programs that support mindfulness are becoming more and more popular for a variety of reasons, including the fact that they support mental and physical health. People are turning to yoga, meditation, and exercise, among other types of physical practice with mindfulness components. Models of psychological therapies are also developing that include more mindfulness strategies as a way of calming the mind and relaxing the body. There are entire centers devoted to teaching mindfulness-based therapies and programs. While mindfulness itself is based in ancient traditions, relaxation techniques have experienced a resurgence in the Western world in recent decades. As they become more popular, there is growing interest in understanding these practices through research.

Most people know someone who says mindfulness is their secret to relaxing and feeling good. Anecdotal evidence to support the benefits of meditation and mindfulness can be found everywhere. Scientists are making discoveries by measuring the effects of mindfulness. To examine the effects of mindfulness, researchers have looked at the effect that practices have on satisfaction, sleep, and stress levels, among other things, using quantifiable biological measurements.

The effects of stress on the body can be monumental. Stress can impact the body's overall function and ability to combat disease. The body has specific hormones that are responsible for the regulation of stress. Cortisol is the essential hormone that keeps the stress response in check. If something is recognized as a threat or stressor, then a hormonal process is triggered within the body by the hypothalamic pituitary adrenal (HPA) axis. This multistep process is what is responsible for the secretion of cortisol. First, a hormone called the corticotropin releasing hormone (CRH) is released by the hypothalamus. Then this hormone travels to the pituitary gland and induces the release of another hormone called the adrenocorticotropin hormone (ACTH), which enters into the bloodstream. Finally, this hormone binds to the adrenal cortex. When this occurs, it then induces secretion of cortisol. This process happens fairly often for everyone, but it becomes a problem when people are not able to come back to a balance and regulation of hormones quickly. The body becomes overstressed when it cannot regulate these hormones properly. Their baseline state becomes an already stressed state. This is what is considered dysregulation of the HPA axis. Essentially, the body becomes stressed so often that it is confused about what constitutes a threat. It also becomes confused about when that threat has passed. When the HPA axis is functioning effectively, it is able to react to stress and then end its reaction swiftly.

Hyperactivity of this stress response is linked to many health-related issues. Some diseases that are related to the immune system, including lupus, chronic fatigue, and multiple sclerosis, have been linked to hyperactivity in the HPA axis. Psychologically, hyperactivity of this stress response is associated with depression. Other diseases such as cardiovascular disease are also related to this dysregulation. In some cases, the hyperactivity of stress can create further illness that then creates greater stress, and so on. It can become a feedback loop with dire consequences.

Mindfulness research has drawn in eminent scientists and medical professionals who seek to understand and prove its benefits. As evidence builds, we will see a major shift in the longstanding beliefs about the division of body and mind. With scientifically quantifiable data, it will be possible to change laws, offer research grants, and bring the benefits of mindfulness to more people.

Researchers are now digging deeper, examining the physiological and biological processes that mindfulness can induce and how they can affect the body. Measuring cortisol levels is a great indicator for effectiveness of mindfulness because it can be more objectively observed and quantified.

One study in 2012 looked at participants who completed a Mindfulness-Based Stress Reduction (MBSR) program offered worldwide. These centers train mental health therapists and facilitators and also offer mindfulness courses and retreats for anyone who is interested. The study gave participants a program that is an eight-week course for people of any background or meditation experience. Participants ranged from new to experienced meditators. Cortisol levels were measured shortly after the body awoke from sleep to compare enduring patterns of cortisol secretion. Cortisol levels present upon awakening were measured and compared between the beginning and end of the course. The results of participating in the eight-week MBSR course demonstrated a positive effect on the body's cortisol secretions. Levels of cortisol were found to decrease for all meditators, new or experienced, when measured at the program's end. This effect was enduring beyond the program's end as well. Other measures showed that sleep had improved significantly by the program's end. The gauge measured how participants reported their ability to fall asleep and to sleep soundly through the night. This is especially important because sleep is a vital component in regulating stress and reproductive hormones and can significantly impact overall health. This could create a feedback loop in which a hyperactive stress response prevents quality sleep that is needed to regulate stress hormones. Through the two markers of stress and sleep, the study showed that mindfulness significantly impacted participants' ability to regulate stress.

A research review titled "Mindfulness and Bodily Distress" (Fjorback 2012) examined in depth four studies that assessed the effects of mindfulness on individuals dealing with bodily distress syndrome. This term is used to capture many disorders that are not easily treated. These disorders are also not well explained by modern medicine. Within this umbrella term are conditions such as fibromyalgia, chronic fatigue syndrome, and irritable bowel syndrome. These are also some of the disorders in most need of research, especially because they are believed to be linked to an overactive and irregular stress response. One study that Fjorback reviewed also used Mindfulness-Based Stress Reduction (MBSR) as well as Mindfulness-Based Cognitive Therapy (MBCT). It compared MBCT to other types of therapy like cognitive behavioral therapy (CBT), which does not have the same mindfulness components. The study used participants' self-report questionnaires to measure their symptoms. The findings of these measures support that mindfulness allowed the participants to recognize when their body was operating in a maladaptive manner. It found that the ability to make the connection between catastrophic thinking and the regulation of the stress response in the nervous system could allow people to begin to use mindfulness to ultimately reduce their symptoms and heal. This is especially important in treating these types of illnesses as people experiencing them typically report not feeling their care is adequate. Participants in these studies often reported resistance to these mindfulness practices because they had been long misunderstood by the medical system and their concerns were dismissed. Mindfulness research can be the bridge from the mind to the body that allows people to begin to scientifically measure the relationship between the mind and body. Participants in these studies were able to understand that, while their health issues did not exist entirely within their mind, it was possible to use the power of their mind and intention to assist the body in healing.

A study by The Chopra Center in 2016 recognized the positive effects of mindfulness on stress-related illnesses and took it one step farther. This deeply biological study looked at the effects of meditation and yoga on a group of women who were not previous meditators and analyzed their blood for improvements on a cellular level.

The scientific community is beginning to make profound discoveries about specific genes. One of these genes is referred to as FOXO3, a gene believed to be directly related to stress. This study considers itself to be the first to present findings that support that intentional stress-reduction intervention can produce positive effects on this specific gene's expression. Because mindfulness can be considered a stress-reduction intervention, this is a huge discovery in favor of mindfulness-related interventions!

This FOXO3 gene is a popular gene in current research. Low levels of this gene diminish behavioral stress and have an antidepressant effect. This is why The Chopra Center study went farther and supported the "meditation effect." Essentially, this has many positive effects on cellular processes, such as the way protein is synthesized and the length of a virus's cycle within the body. This is another great piece of evidence because it means that mindfulness has an actual antiviral effect on the body. This incredible finding by The Chopra Center uses measurements of gene expression, "bio-markers," to quantify the effects of meditation. The Center looked at other bio-markers, such as ratios within the plasma of the blood, for information. In these findings, meditation affected the blood plasma ratio, altering it to a specific ratio that existing research already believed to be connected to a lowered risk of developing dementia. Another specific plasma ratio documented that meditation reduced risks related to depression, dementia, and higher mortality rates. Studying and researching these bio-markers in relation to mindfulness is important work.

The Chopra Center used this study to compare the effect of a meditation and yoga retreat to a retreat or vacation without a mindfulness component. There were no differences in the initial findings. Both groups had similar effects in the gene expressions and blood plasma ratio. However, after returning to their normal routine, the participants in the vacation group did not experience the enduring effects that those in the meditation group did.

It is an exciting time for the growing body of mindfulness research. There is a lot of concrete evidence that supports the value of teaching mindfulness, especially as a skill that could be incorporated into school curriculums. It has been shown that these tools can improve overall health. It has also been shown that once these tools have been learned, their positive effects can endure longer than other methods of relaxation. The more research and support that goes into the field of mindfulness, the more it is understood from a scientific perspective. You can keep up to date as this body of research continues to grow, and you can begin to experiment in your own life right away—with this very breath!

5

mindfulness and the brain

For all human beings, everything begins and ends with the brain. Every move we make, every instinct we have, every problem we solve, every complicated emotional scenario we could conjure, every moment of joy, and every moment of pain are the result of the interplay between our brain, our body, and the world around us. That's why our thoughts truly shape our reality. When we understand the power of our brain we have the opportunity to harness it.

The function of our brain can seem tremendously complex, considering the different lobes that regulate different aspects of behavior, memory, learning, emotion, creativity, motor function, social interaction, and planning, among other things, and the brain's beautifully efficient system of neurotransmitters. Neurotransmitters are chemical messengers that transfer information from one part of the body to another. With all of these chemical impulses bouncing around the body and the complicated and amazing arrangement of cells within us, it is not surprising that sometimes things go a bit awry when we throw in our fast-paced, modern lives. Enter mindfulness, the elixir of peace and calm.

Mindfulness is the ongoing practice of using your awareness to connect with the present moment. Research supports that this practice enhances ability to regulate thoughts and emotions. Mindfulness has been practiced for thousands of years in different cultures and civilizations to regulate the mind and body. At a time when mental disorders such as anxiety and depression have a higher prevalence than previously documented, it is vital for us to look at how mindfulness can assist in regulating mood.

New programs and styles of therapy using mindfulness are emerging to treat disorders such as anxiety and depression. They are built on the belief that meditation is a crucial component to mental health. As these new styles of therapy become more known, there is a growing body of research to support them. However, few studies look at the specific hormonal and neurotransmitter processes that occur in the brain during experiences of anxiety and depression. Even fewer studies examine the effects of meditation and other mindfulness practices on the states of anxiety and depression from a neurological and biological lens.

A study from the University of Utah looked at yoga and meditation as treatment for anxiety and depression. It found that yoga positively impacted participants' stress responses and assisted in alleviating symptoms of anxiety and depression. An overactive stress response can lead to consistently higher levels of cortisol, an important stress hormone that can become dysregulated. By regulating this stress response, individuals can reduce their heart rate and improve their breathing.

The study also found that if a person has a dysregulated stress response, that person also has increased sensitivity to pain. This is important to note as there are many stress-related illnesses that are not well understood—like fibromyalgia—that often correlate with mental health disorders such as anxiety and depression. As yoga is increasingly scientifically researched, it becomes more apparent that physical and psychological benefits enhance one another. If you assist with one, you will naturally help yourself with the other as well.

Some studies have looked at mindfulness practices, such as Mindfulness-Based Cognitive Therapy (MBCT), as treatment for depression. This type of therapy has been found to help people become aware of their thought patterns and ultimately decrease their depressive symptoms, suggesting that this can even help to prevent the onset of a depressive episode. Mindfulness practices can be useful tools for maintaining mental health.

Many of the studies compared treatments like these to antidepressant medications. Antidepressants are pharmacological interventions that aim to regulate the brain's hormones, called neurotransmitters, that are believed to play a critical role in disorders such as anxiety and depression. One drawback to pharmacological intervention is the numerous side effects that may result from these medications. Mindfulness and meditation have no known negative side effects.

Many believe that depression is caused by a dysregulation of neurotransmitters such as serotonin, dopamine, norepinephrine, and even oxytocin. This is supported by research, but there remains some skepticism and disagreement within the mental health field about how these neurotransmitters can be best regulated.

The fact is, modern medicine does not have conclusive evidence about these neurotransmitters' specific role in depression and anxiety. It is not certain how or why antidepressants work, and many studies show placebo effects and therapy to have similar effects to antidepressants. Countless studies support their success, but it still remains a mystery what exact levels of which hormones create the desired or balanced state to optimize mental health. Serotonin is specifically supported in some studies to be related to mood regulation and mental health. Serotonin binds to a few different receptors in the brain, and one study in Simon Young's review showed higher levels of binding potential in brain scans of depressed individuals. At the time of this review in 2011, Young found that no studies had looked at the specific effect of MBCT or any other mindfulness-based practices on specific serotonin receptor functioning. This is an area for research that still desperately needs attention, as mindfulness could be further legitimatized in modern medicine with evidence like this. Studies already support that MBCT helps to change the dysregulation of thoughts and emotions associated with depression, but there is not a direct measure of the neurotransmitters that are believed to be associated with these dysregulations. Many believe that science needs to continue to measure biological markers to be able to make changes in treatment of mental disorders. It is common knowledge that it is difficult to change things such as education and treatment preferences without evidence-based concrete treatments. While anti-depressants work wonderfully for some, many people are resistant to this type of intervention and others who try many different medications do not find relief. Mindfulness may be the missing component to their treatment.

A 2003 study examined the biological components of meditation. Participants were split into two groups: one completed an eight-week training program in meditation and the other did not. This study also looked at participants' immune functioning by administering the flu vaccine to participants in the meditation and control groups. Anxiety in the participants was measured using questionnaires, and electroencephalograph (EEG) brain scans were made of their brains to assess different levels of activity. The study found that the meditation group had higher levels of left-side anterior activation in the brain. The activation of the left-side anterior region of the brain is associated with the way emotions are processed and regulated. Previous reviews by Davidson (2000) found that a greater level of left-side anterior activation is associated with quicker recovery from perceived negative emotional states. This means meditation was shown to affect the brain in a way that allows a person to deal with stress and difficult emotions more effectively, recovering faster from aroused emotional states. This is very important to consider when looking at anxiety and depressive disorders, as people struggling with these issues often find they become stuck in maladaptive patterns of thinking or experience intense and enduring emotional states. The study also supported better immune functioning, which can have many implications. A lowered immunity is linked to development of many physical illnesses that, as earlier mentioned, can be argued to always be directly connected to brain and mental health.

While understanding how meditation changes neurological processes is still developing, as is our understanding of the brain itself, it is not disputed within the research that meditation does indeed change the brain. Many recent studies, including one in 2000 (by Lazar et al) suggest that functional magnetic resonance imaging (rs-fMRI) clearly showed the effect of meditation on the brain. This specific study looked at depressed individuals' brains after a period of guided meditation to induce body-mind relaxation. The brain scans actually showed increased connectivity between prefrontal nodes. The prefrontal nodes are believed to be responsible for behavioral planning, decision making, future goals, memories of the self, and many other processes. They have been linked to anxiety and depression. The findings of these rs-fMRIs mean that meditation could positively impact the ability of the depressed brain to use reasoning and self-soothing by means of the functions of the prefrontal nodes. People's ability to separate themselves from their maladaptive narratives about their past could be positively affected. This makes complete sense when we think about mindfulness and its aim to stay with the present moment, detaching from old narratives or stories, and breaking unhelpful patterns of thinking or behaving. Again, the mental process undertaken seems to mirror the neurological processes, at least from first glance and with the limited understanding of the brain that we have.

The journal *Mindfulness* released a study in 2010 that discusses and critiques the growing desire for scientific research to capture the brain's neurological and biological responses to meditation. While eager scientists attempt to essentially reduce the effects of the meditation and mindfulness using a limited understanding propelled by neuroscience, mindfulness experts believe that this may not be possible. Given the complexity of its effects, meditation can be examined through many different lenses. It alters the brain and body's hormones and processes. It is shown to regulate stress. Using an analysis of the brain to describe meditation's impact is limiting, given its profound and even spiritual nature. For example, Fletcher et al. talks about using meditation to increase levels of compassion. Meditation has been shown to increase levels of oxytocin, a neuropeptide that is related to feelings of connectedness to others and happiness. Oxytocin is released when we hug or kiss someone or when we interact with our loved ones. This study says that we cannot use neuroimaging of the brain to provide concrete evidence of the experience of compassion. The relationship between oxytocin and compassion can be correlated, but in science, correlation is not equal to causation. The mental process that a person undergoes when meditating—specifically in a compassion meditation—can be observed in more than just the brain. It is a bigger psychological and, some would argue, spiritual process that allows a person to understand the connection and non-separateness from others. These processes can have profound effects on symptoms of anxiety and depression, and these processes may not be able to be truly observed by brain imaging alone.

Deepak Chopra, MD, has spent a lot of his life researching and writing about the benefits of meditation and spirituality, using his medical degree to inform his perspective. He states that "meditation triggers the brain to release neurotransmitters, including dopamine, serotonin, oxytocin, and endorphins." He goes on to link each of these neurotransmitters to happiness and overall well-being. He cites many of the studies reviewed earlier that have measured lowered anxiety and depression in participants after completing meditation programs and therapies. He also cites studies that have shown decreased experiences of pain. The correlations between the studies that show the role of neurotransmitters with anxiety and depression and the studies that show the effectiveness of meditation support his claim. Chopra asserts that while the exact causes of depression are unclear, it is a result of some kind of imbalance. This imbalance can be biological, psychological, emotional, or physical—it is not known. He calls meditation the "birthplace of happiness," because "silence is the birthplace of happiness." When we can sit in silence, we can separate from all the mental chatter that is often related to and creating our feelings. Brain scans show that simply thinking of a loved one, or a traumatic memory, can alter the hormones and functioning of our brains. This means that if the mind can create silence and ground into the present moment, a person can become separate from these emotions. He also asserts that the experience of meditation becomes profound, creating an awareness of the divinity of existence.

The effect of mindfulness on the brain is only beginning to be better understood and is an area for exciting new research. Possibly the more that is discovered, the more will be understood about the process. It is also possible that the more that is learned, the more mysterious the process will become. What is certain is that many people are experiencing profound benefits from mindfulness that can be measured not only in their report of their quality of life but also objectively within the brain.

6

types of mindfulness practice

Mindfulness can take many forms. Whether you are a beginner or an expert, you will find many types of mindfulness that can expand your awareness. Mindful practices such as meditation and yoga have been scientifically proven to improve physical health, reduce anxiety, and enhance happiness. So, wherever you are on your journey, even if you've never practiced mindfulness before, try one of these relaxing exercises today.

Mini-moments of mindfulness practice can be done any time throughout the day and require no special training or ability. They are a great place to start for beginners who want to incorporate mindfulness in small pieces.

MINDFUL SEEING

Not all mindful activities require closing your eyes—in fact, some people may feel more comfortable being able to take in visual stimuli while they meditate. The only requirement for mindful seeing is a window with a view. Do this meditation for ten to twenty minutes. These are the five steps to mindful seeing:

1. Find a comfortable place in front of a window with a view.

2. Carefully observe everything while looking out the window. Try not to label what you see. Instead, simply notice colors, patterns, and textures.

3. Pay attention to anything that moves—wind blowing leaves, people walking, birds flying, for example. Pay attention to the many different shapes you can see through the window. Let yourself view everything from the perspective of someone unfamiliar with what you are seeing.

4. Be closely observant but do not judge what you see. Don't fixate on or critique the sights you see. Simply be aware of them.

5. Any time your attention strays, redirect it nonjudgmentally by noticing another color or movement. Don't let distractions pull you away from observing, just gently pull your mind back.

THE BLUEBERRY EXERCISE

The blueberry exercise is a great beginner's mindfulness practice. Usually, a facilitator or teacher provides students with a blueberry and requests that they pretend they have never seen a blueberry before. The teacher tells students to pay close attention to how the blueberry looks, how it feels in their hands, how the blueberry skin changes after being touched and held, how it smells, and how it tastes. By focusing on a single, small object, students use this mindfulness practice to help focus on what's in front of them and give all their attention to the present moment. The blueberry exercise forces practitioners to stay in the moment completely.

LOVING-KINDNESS MEDITATION

Loving-kindness is a mindfulness practice that connects practitioners to the outside world by sending and receiving love. The steps of a short loving-kindness meditation follow:

1. Close your eyes, sit in a comfortable position with your back upright, and relax your body. Focus inward. Take a deep breath in and then back.

2. To receive loving kindness, think of someone who loves you and cares about you. It could be anyone in your life, past or present. Imagine that person on your right, sending you love, and feel the warmth and goodwill coming from him or her. Do the same thing, this time imagining a different person who loves you on your left. Then move outward, imagining you are surrounded by people who care for you on all sides. Bask in the warmth of this feeling.

3. To send loving-kindness, bring your attention back to the first person you visualized on your right side. Start to send the positivity you feel back to that person. You can repeat the following mantra to send loving-kindness:

MAY ALL PEOPLE BE HAPPY.

MAY ALL PEOPLE BE FREE.

MAY ALL PEOPLE BE HEALTHY.

MAY ALL PEOPLE BE AT PEACE.

4. A good order for your mindfulness practice is to send loving-kindness to those you love, then to send it to a neutral person you may visualize, and to finish your exercise, send it to all beings in the world.

BODY-SCAN MEDITATION

Popularized by Jon Kabat-Zinn, founder of the MBSR movement, a body scan is a simple but effective way to practice mindfulness. It is accessible to beginners and does not require much time. The body scan moves through each region of the body and asks participants to pay special attention to how the parts of their body are feeling. The scan traditionally moves from the toes up to the legs, pelvic region, abdomen, chest, back, shoulders, hands, arms, neck, and face/head. There are five main steps that meditation leaders will walk participants through:

1. Participants are asked to lie on their backs with their palms facing the ceiling and their feet placed slightly apart. If any participants are unable to lie down, they can sit in a comfortable chair with their feet solidly on the floor.

2. Participants are asked to remain very still for the duration of the exercise and to move only if necessary and with awareness of their movements.

3. Participants begin with a guided portion of the body scan. First, they are asked to bring awareness to their breathing and observe the way their breath flows in and out. By noticing the rhythm of breath, participants usually relax into their breathing more fully. The goal in breath awareness is not to change the way participants are breathing but to hold gentle awareness of it. As participants relax, their breath will likely change and become deeper and steadier naturally.

4. Next, participants begin to pay attention their body: how their clothes feel against their skin, how the surface they are sitting on or lying on feels, how the temperature of the room affects them, and what is going on in the environment around them.

5. Last, a facilitator can guide participant awareness to any particular parts of the body that call attention to themselves—these could be places that are sore or feel very heavy or light or perhaps are tingling. Participants can bring awareness upward from the toes to the legs, pelvic region, abdomen, chest, back, and shoulders, and then to the hands, arms, neck, and face/head. Participants are asked to note places where they may not feel anything at all or, on the other end of the spectrum, that are greatly sensitive.

Once participants have completed the scan, they can come back in the room by slowly opening their eyes and moving to a comfortable sitting position.

TONGLEN

Tonglen is a Tibetan Buddhist meditation practice that literally translates to "giving and taking." The practice was originally described in seven steps and is attributed to an Indian Buddhist teacher, Atisha Dipankara Shrijnana. Langri Tangpa wrote them down for the first time in the eleventh century. The practice involves breathing exercises you can perform while sitting and that are used to purify your karma by giving, training you in altruism, and reducing selfish attachment. During your practice, breathe in and visualize taking in others' suffering as well as your own. This suffering can be about a particular group of people, a specific country, or even just one person. When you breathe out, you should give recognition and compassion to all living beings. Pema Chödrön, well-known American Buddhist nun and author, instructs practitioners to breathe out and hold space for others' hearts and minds to feel great enough to live with their discomfort and suffering. She suggests that if your practice is for those without food, breathe out food. If your practice is for those without homes, breathe out shelter. The in breath is your wish to take away suffering, and the out breath is your wish to send comfort and happiness to the same people (or countries, animals, etc.). The idea behind tonglen is that practitioners can develop and expand their loving kindness.

The following types of mindfulness practice can help to soothe your mind but do so through thoughtful physical activity.

Don't be taken aback by the fact that they are exercises—all three can be scaled back for beginners and offer various levels of intensity.

QIGONG

Qigong is an ancient Chinese exercise and health system that involves body posture, movement, breathing, and meditation. It began as a traditional philosophy for spiritual well-being but has transitioned into a health and mindfulness exercise as well. The first step of qigong is to train your breathing and focus on a relaxed, rhythmic breathing pattern. Qigong also encourages the stretching of your breath, which means holding your inhales and exhales to expand them. Qigong has mental elements and instills the importance for all practitioners of settling the mind and relaxing physically and mentally. There are specific sets of movements that can be completed in qigong, as well as various postures (standing, sitting, lying down) for those who wish to delve deeper into the practice.

TAI CHI

Tai chi is another ancient Chinese exercise, actually a martial art form that is sometimes called meditation in motion. It promotes relaxation, stress relief, lowered anxiety, and heightened awareness. Tai chi practices are a series of slow, methodical movements that are low impact and can be incorporated into any mindfulness routine.

The most important step in tai chi is warming up the body, which also promotes mental relaxation. A good place to begin is with a loosening-up exercise. While standing with your feet parallel, you can relax your arms at your sides and begin rotating to the left and right, allowing your arms to hang loosely. This can be expanded to your neck, shoulders, and spine so that your whole body begins to warm up before you move into the exercise regimen.

One of the most basic tai chi movements that encourages flexibility is "the windmill." With your feet placed apart and parallel, relax your shoulders and point your fingers toward the floor. On the inhale, bring your arms over your head straight above your shoulders and stretch toward the ceiling while arching your back. On the exhale, bend forward slowly and move your hands down the midline of your body. Then bend forward from the hips and allow your arms to hang loosely in front of you. When you inhale again, return to your starting position.

7

watching the inner show

As you begin to live a mindful lifestyle, you may become aware of the most entertaining soap opera you have ever witnessed—right inside of your own mind. Each moment of every day we are barraged by an inner monologue narrating what's happening to us in the present moment. But this inner narrator gets easily distracted. So, let's say a man tastes a food that reminds him of a family dinner five years before. Then he begins thinking about that and how at that dinner there was a big disagreement and it was stressful. It's as if he's reexperiencing it in the present moment—even if just for a few seconds. How and why do our minds jump around? Why are we narrating our everyday experience and punctuating it with drama?

For example, perhaps a woman hears a song the next evening that reminds her of a past love. Maybe it brings her mind down a train of thought all about how that relationship didn't work, and she begins replaying scenes from it in her mind. She feels the emotions again. She has the thoughts again and then adds to them. She takes up a lot of mental and emotional space thinking about the past and feeling it. Is she doing so at the expense of experiencing the present?

When we think about something, our brain and body do much of what they would do if we were actually experiencing that same thing. So, we release the same or similar chemical messengers to tell us what to feel. When you remember an embarrassing situation where your face turned bright red and you started sweating, does your body start sweating and does your face turn red? Just by thinking about it? Often times it does. Chemical messengers similar to those released when you actually had the experience are racing through your bloodstream and giving your body directions how to physiologically react.

Every day, we watch an inner show of ups and downs, highs and lows, joys and turmoil. It's an endless dance of existence. But it's possible to bring a little mindfulness into this dance. What if we were simply present for these ups and downs and highs and lows? Especially since the majority of them are self-generated within the mind. What if we brought our attention to our "inner witness" instead of staying on the internal emotional roller coaster?

The inner witness is a part of us that sits behind all of the drama. It observes our personality with detachment. Please do not mistake detachment for lack of care, because the inner witness observes with unconditional love and acceptance, but is not attached to outcomes in this world. Instead, it sits quietly being present and simply is. It is the part of us that is able to just be.

So, what if you could relax your heart and quiet your mind enough to lean back into the awareness of that inner witness? Perhaps you could slide back out of the drama for a few seconds. Might that be a relief at times?

If you practice mindfulness, you can extend those times and their frequency. Being present with your inner witness simply requires a shift in attention. It's kind of like changing the lens with which you view the world. For example, right now you're reading these words. And in your mind, they're being narrated by your inner voice. Notice that right now as you're reading. That's the voice in your head! That's the voice that generates all of the drama. Drama means the drama, the inner conflict that the inner voice creates with our mind. So we are getting behind the drama we create in our mind and instead of witnessing it, as opposed to feeling it, it *is* us. It's the voice that says, "Did I remember to turn off the stove?" "Did I remember to add laundry detergent when I started the washing machine?" "I hope Jennifer didn't take what I said out of context."

What you want to do is get behind and watch your inner dialogue instead of feeling like you're living within it and that it is your only experience. The voice of your inner narrator is just a portion of the vast collection of parts that make up your complete being. Yes, your "personality self" is in there. And try as it might, it cannot monopolize all of your attention if you don't let it. Your personality self's job is to make your world understandable. As a result, it's going to try to compare and contrast every experience with every other experience you've had. It's going to try to categorize what you're doing as positive or negative.

Your personality self is what is passing judgment on what you liked and didn't like about what happened on any given day. By nature, your personality self wants to control your experience to make it more pleasant and less dangerous.

It likely originated as we evolved as a species. Because we were under greater strain and our survival was threatened more frequently, we developed a willful brain that would try its hardest to minimize risk and increase reward.

For many of us in the Western world, we are no longer likely to be under attack at any given moment. And we're not in aggressive competition for resources either. Most of us have what we need. Therefore, the personality develops in different ways but with the same impetus—how to be most secure, whether physically, emotionally, mentally, or even spiritually. That search for security might translate into ways that you choose to guard your heart and emotions in romantic relationships. Or it might translate into unconscious competitive feelings with coworkers.

Sometimes our personality self is very helpful. It's something that we need. The way we are as individuals is part of why we are successful, and why we have formed the relationships we have. But, because it isn't the only part of us, then why should it be the only part of our experience?

You are a vast being. And, yes, you have a personality self in this body within this construct of time and space. But you also have many other parts that are infinite. One of these is your inner witness.

When you are busy, just noticing the busyness is an act of mind-fulness. Your inner witness is what allows you to be mindful. It sits behind the chatter and the day-to-day activity and simply observes. When you sit in meditation, you can allow yourself to relax more deeply and let your mind chatter subside. Then if you just sit back in yourself a little bit you can begin to feel what's behind your per-sonality self. Relax your heart and feel that behind all of the mind chatter is your silent inner-witness presence. It is pure peace and it is your divine soul—that part of you that is eternally mindful. It is eternally present. It is the part of you that existed before you entered the body you are inhabiting, and it will exist after you exit that body. When you meditate and slow down your mind, you give yourself an opportunity to rest a little farther back in your consciousness and experience the awareness of your inner witness. Let a mindful life spring forth from the part of you that simply witnesses your life without judgment.

8

mindfulness meditations

Today we live in a fast-paced, hectic world. We are frequently bombarded with overwhelming stimuli. We have more people in our lives than ever. We have more friends, more family we're in touch with, more contacts for work. This could be because of social media and also because of all of our expanded technological capabilities. When life is this frenetic you can't help but wonder, what effects does this have on your health and state of mind? Are your mental and emotional health affected by potential stress caused by a busy life? Your physical health likely may be affected as well. We may not be able to escape the stress of modern life completely, but we can develop coping mechanisms that help us mitigate that stress and bring positive emotions and experiences into our reality. Our intention shall be to allow ourselves rest and relaxation in ample quantity and of a high quality amidst a joyful and fulfilling life filled with passion and love.

In the following section, you'll find an array of mindfulness meditations to help you center yourself and develop a relaxed yet focused mind. Meditation is our number one tool in the quest for greater mindfulness. The scientific benefits of meditation have been confirmed in numerous studies, as has been mentioned earlier. The spiritual benefits of meditation are much discussed among yogis and enthusiasts. But be aware, too, of the emotional benefits of meditation. When we meditate, we quiet the mind and give ourselves a break from the roller coaster of emotions.

When we are mindful, we are simply noticing, and we rarely get wrapped up in the drama within ourselves. Yes, we are all human beings. And no matter how much we meditate or how mindful we are, there will be times when we lose ourselves. We might lose our center but even that is temporary, as all things are. With consistent meditation practice we have the ability to bring ourselves back to center. With practice, it becomes a path we have walked many times. It's well worn, and we know how to get back home within ourselves. So, use this selection of meditations to find your own internal home—one filled with calm, quiet, and mindfulness.

WALKING MINDFULLY

Mindfulness is about staying grounded in the present moment. This idea of mindfulness is becoming more popular because staying present can be a challenge nowadays. We are bombarded with stimuli from all directions, causing our minds to anticipate and react to each stimulus. Mindfulness allows us to bring our attention to what is happening now. Mindfulness research suggests that this practice reduces stress and disease while increasing positive emotions and overall life satisfaction.

Walking Mindfully Meditation

A walking meditation is particularly helpful in cultivating mindfulness because it includes an active physical process. This type of meditation allows us to focus our awareness on physical sensations. We are able to anchor to each present moment as we intentionally step with our feet and observe this physical act. Many find that it is transformational to bring awareness to a task that we do without awareness most of the time. It can allow us to extend this type of mindfulness into our everyday life when we are walking to and from the places we need to be.

Practicing this type of mindful walking may allow us to achieve a true state of meditation in which thoughts cease. When the mind achieves this state, we are left in mental stillness while physically walking and mentally observing this process. This type of meditation is great for beginner meditators or those people who find it extremely challenging to stay present while sitting still. Many individuals who experience an overactive mind or restless body may find this meditation to be effective.

Walking meditation has been incorporated into mindfulness programs with great success. The Mindfulness-Based Stress Reduction (MBSR) Program includes walking meditation as an integral part of its eight-week program. The program has been shown to be powerful at enhancing quality of life and reducing negative symptoms in participants experiencing physical or mental illnesses such as cancer or depression. It works to allow you to really become mindful.

Walking is done so often in a rushed and absentminded state. We usually concentrate on the destination rather than the process of getting there. By bringing awareness to walking, we can change the way our brain perceives the internal and external stimuli that come up as we walk. We begin to notice more of what is happening within us and around us. A natural by-product of mindful walking meditation is an increased mastery of our feelings and thoughts. Such mastery ultimately allows us to better control our actions and responses to negative or intense emotions.

Walking Meditation

Set aside some time to complete this meditation, preferably at least ten minutes. Locate an area where you can walk around safely. You may choose to pace back and forth, meander, or create a circuit that you can walk around. Try to locate an area where it will be unlikely you will encounter another person who will try to talk to you. If you can find a private area, this is best.

You can walk inside if you have space to do so or outside in nature. Create the intention to be mindful of your walking. You are not focused on the destination. You are present with the journey. The following are the steps to take during a walking meditation:

1. Begin walking. As you begin to walk, you can focus your awareness on your breath. Observe any sounds you may hear. Now begin to notice each step. Begin to notice each part of the step. Consciously notice these actions that are usually completed automatically and unconsciously.

2. Observe your body as you pick up your foot. Feel the muscles in the foot and leg engage and disengage. Notice the floor or ground underneath the lifted foot. Notice the foot move away from your body. Notice the muscles engage. Observe your foot as you place it down. Lead this movement with the heel touching down first. Notice any sensations that arise in the foot or anywhere else in the body as you place the foot down. Notice the ground beneath your foot. Notice anything you may hear or feel. Observe your body shift its weight onto the leg that has been placed forward. Feel the muscles engage. Notice the back leg as the foot begin to lift. Allow the heel to lift first before lifting the whole foot. Notice the heel lift. Notice the toes lift. Observe any sounds or any feelings as this occurs. Observe your foot as it completely lifts and begins to move upward and forward. Notice the foot lower to the ground. Notice the heel touch the ground. Notice the whole foot settle onto the ground. Feel the shift in your weight as you move toward the next step.

3. Continue to mentally observe each individual part of each step. Use your attention and awareness to stay completely present with each movement. Notice if your mind wanders. Do not judge this or yourself. You are not the mind. Do not resist the mind. Simply notice it and bring it back. Use your senses to ground yourself back in this moment. Use your awareness. Notice your breath.

4. Walk without rushing. Slow movements are best in order to allow you to mindfully observe each segment of each step. Take small steps but allow the movement to come naturally without forcing or changing it too much. Allow your hands and arms to relax in whatever way feels most comfortable. If allowing them to hang feels right, then allow that. Observe the movement in your hands and arms. If holding the hands together behind your back feels natural, do so as it may allow you to completely focus on the steps instead of your swaying hands.

5. As you walk, focus on different sensations. Notice the crunch of the ground under your foot. Notice your breath. Focus on your legs and each muscle that engages with each step. Notice your upper body and how it feels.

Use your other senses. What do you see? What do you hear? What can you smell?

6. You may find you want to use a mantra or affirmation to focus your attention. A great mantra for walking meditation is "So hum," which in Sanskrit simply means "I am that." As you look around and notice the environment you walk within, you remind yourself that you are not separate from what is around you. As you breathe in, you can say "So," and as you breathe out, "hum."

7. Practice walking mindfully often. Notice yourself walking in your everyday life. Notice the sensations that you are often unconscious of. Notice your surroundings. Let these sensations anchor you back into this present moment.

DRINKING AND EATING MINDFULLY

Eating mindfully is incredibly powerful. Many have complicated relationships with food. We are often eating while stressed and rushing from one activity to the next. Physically, stressed or rushed eating is challenging for our bodies. If we are rushed or stressed, our bodies are using energy to hold tension and activate our stress responses. This means that the energy used to hold tension in our body can cause us to digest our food improperly. Then in turn can contribute to digestive issues and immune diseases. As you eat, you should be chewing your food very thoroughly. Chewing assiduously is the first step in digestion and the most commonly neglected. We need to produce copious amounts of saliva during this stage to assist the body in proper digestion. Many people do not realize that drinking quickly—even healthy smoothies—may not allow you to absorb all of the nutrients. That is why some dieticians recommend you chew your smoothie. When you drink a smoothie, take the time to chew it. Taste the flavors of the smoothie and allow your senses to come alive. During this process, your mouth will salivate and assist in proper digestion.

We often do not take time to appreciate and love our food. By intentionally loving our food and putting a positive intention into absorbing what we are eating, we are ultimately giving ourselves more energy from our food. Mindless eating means that we are detached from our food and our hunger indicators and are not present with our body or food. It is much more common to see mindless eating than mindful eating. In fact, it is often encouraged within our culture to eat mindlessly. We go out for dinner and chat with our friends without taking the time to tune in with our bodies. This can lead to overeating and ignoring the indicators that our body gives us when we are full. We should aim for eating to live, rather than living to eat.

We often choose to eat in an attempt to fill an emotional void. Sometimes we are not consciously choosing to eat. We simply find ourselves eating without intentionally choosing it. Instead of noticing hunger, we notice sadness or sometimes boredom. Because we naturally get a surge of dopamine when we eat, we are drawn to food. Eating makes us feel good. But there are healthier ways to achieve this same feeling other than mindless eating.

When we eat while we do other things, we are also eating mindlessly. Many of us eat our lunch at our desk or while browsing social media. This is not eating mindfully. We become disconnected from the sensations of tasting and digesting.

Mindful eating is partially about consciously choosing what you will eat. It is about stopping when cravings hit to consider the choice to eat or not. It is about listening to what the body needs and honoring that. If you are hungry, eat. If you are not, then don't. Slow down and let the body have time to communicate what you need as you eat. Think about choosing to eat a blueberry muffin. First you notice you are hungry and craving something sweet. You pass ice cream stores and fast-food restaurants. You notice an organic bakery. You choose to give your body something sweet that also has nutrients, so you enter the organic bakery. You notice a blueberry muffin made from locally sourced blueberries and sweetened with maple syrup. You choose to buy the muffin because you believe it is the healthiest choice for your body. You look at the muffin. You notice the swirls of blue and how different areas of the muffin are baked. You thank the people who have prepared the muffin, including those who grew the ingredients that are in it. You break open the muffin. You notice the texture as you do so. You smell the aroma of maple syrup, blueberries, and fresh bread. You take one bite and notice your mouth light up with excitement. With gratitude, you slowly chew and experience each bite. You intentionally choose when to swallow. You notice the muffin travel into your esophagus and downward into your stomach. You take your time to eat the muffin in this manner until you notice your stomach beginning to feel full. If you notice you are full before you finish the muffin, give yourself the opportunity to save the rest for later when your body cues you that you are hungry once again.

Eating mindfully is something you can do at every meal. Eating can become a meditation when you sit down to refuel your body with food or drink.

Mindful Eating Meditation

1. First notice when your body is signaling that you are hungry. Take a few deep breaths. Notice these sensations and understand that they are hunger cues. Breathe and accept this feeling. Do not react by eating immediately when you notice hunger. Then choose to nourish yourself with healthy food.

2. Become aware of the food choices you have. Notice the thoughts and feelings that come up as you consider these choices. Stop yourself and breathe. Make a choice that is aligned with what your body needs based on your energy level, intensity of hunger, and activities planned for the day. Notice which choices arise only as emotional comfort.

3. Prepare your food mindfully, or if the food is being prepared for you, consider the preparation of the food and visualize this process. In either case, consider how the food gets to your plate. Consider where it came from and how.

4. Notice the textures in the food. As you prepare your food, mindfully cut each vegetable or remove each wrapper with care and intentionality. Notice each sense as you smell, observe, and feel the food during preparation. Notice your mouth begin to salivate as you prepare to eat.

5. Sit down at a designated place to eat. Set your food in front of you and take a moment to connect with your meal. See the colors and shapes of your food. Set aside any distractions. Turn off the TV. Put away your phone. Sit comfortably but with good posture. Connect with your breath. Enjoy the silence.

6. Place the first bite into your mouth. Focus your awareness on your senses of smell, taste, and touch as the food touches your tongue. Begin to chew and continue to breathe.

7. Chew all the food in your mouth thoroughly before choosing a time to swallow. Try to create space between chewing and the intention to swallow. Try to transform swallowing from an unconscious reflex to an intentional process.

8. Stay present. Use your breath. If you are creating mental lists or are absent from the moment, unconscious patterns of eating will reemerge. Do not judge yourself if this happens. Bring yourself back using your breath and the awareness of your senses.

9. Check in with your body to notice cues for fullness. If your stomach feels three-quarters full, then this a good time to stop eating. Do not let the amount of food in front of you determine how much you eat. Let your body indicate what it needs and when it needs it.

10. As you finish eating, notice the tastes that linger in your mouth. Notice the fullness in your body. Notice any changes from previous meals and make a mental note of hunger and fullness cues that may be new to you.

11. Continue these practices. If possible, practice daily for twenty-one days. Many yogis and mindfulness practitioners believe it takes this long to form new habits. The more you practice mindfulness in daily activities such as walking and eating, the more naturally it will occur. Mindfulness will be present. You will find yourself slowing down your mind to truly experience your life. When you experience this shift, you will not want to go back to multitasking while eating or walking. You may find that you will accomplish more by focusing on each task wholly and mindfully. Through mindful eating, you may find yourself becoming healthier, losing weight, and developing better digestion. If you already have a meditation practice, you may find these specific practices enhance your overall ability to meditate. Use these meditations to connect with your body and realize the subtle messages your body is giving that you often miss in your daily life.

MINDFUL EMOTIONS

In this meditation, we will journey deeply within the emotional body. That's the part of our being woven through our physical body that encompasses our emotions and their energy. Our physical bodies are knit with electromagnetic energy. This is often referred to as the body's aura. It is a scientific fact that our bodies are full of electromagnetic energy and that we have an electromagnetic field around us. The field is easily measurable.

Part of the neutral energy contained in this field is what holds together the energy of our emotions. Our emotions are generated within our mind and through the complex symphony of brain and body chemicals. The emotions that we experience also have electromagnetic energy and the universal life force that permeates our physical body and our being.

In fact, we are all multidimensional beings. We exist in the physical dimension, and we also exist in our own internal emotional worlds. These parts of us interact with the invisible energy world that is interwoven with all existence. That invisible energy world is comprised of a universal life force. This is a clear, clean, neutral energy that enlivens all existence. Some people like to personify this energy as love or light. It's all of these things and more. It's the universality that weaves us together.

Endeavoring to be mindful in our emotional life is probably the biggest challenge for human beings. As humans, we are an emotional bunch! No matter whether we repress emotions or are exquisitely in tune with them, we are governed by them in large portions of our lives. So, to bring the skill of being mindful into our emotional experience is a useful way to become more self-actualized. It also brings us a sense of calm and tranquility that we often crave, especially when our emotions are agitated.

For this meditation, we will call on the assistance of an ancient Taoist goddess named Chang-Er. In Chinese mythology, she is thought to live within the moon and to be a nurturing and caring presence. She is uniquely attuned to our emotions and also incredibly adept at helping us navigate their symbolism while easily surfing their ebbs and flows.

Emotional Calm Meditation

1. Take a few minutes to relax. Close your eyes and spend some time being mindful of your breath. Allow yourself to enter a meditative state. When you have quieted your mind enough that you are beginning to feel space between your thoughts, begin the following process.

2. Bring your attention to the center of your chest. This is the place where many cultures and philosophies believe that the energy of your heart resides. This energy center is an origin point for universal love.

3. As you center your attention in your chest, allow yourself to feel a pulsing sensation there. Allow yourself to imagine that universal love energy is pulsing.

4. This will be the access point from which you will process and integrate your emotions today. As you keep your attention centered in your chest, say aloud or in your mind, "For my highest good and the highest good of all life, I call upon Chang Er to help me balance and integrate my emotions so I may live in ever-growing harmony and joy."

5. Now rest with your eyes closed and place your hands in the following mudra (a hand movement, position, or gesture used in ceremonies and yoga to enhance meditation; each mudra has a specific meaning and can be healing or bring a particular energetic vibration): connect the tips of your thumbs with the outermost knuckle of your ring fingers on the side closest to your middle fingers.

6. Inhale deeply through your nose and bring air all the way down into your abdomen, filling it completely. Place your tongue on the roof of your mouth. Exhale the air through your mouth in a steady slow stream, as if you are blowing the breath through a straw. Do this two more times.

7. Gently tap the point three times where your thumbs are resting. Now with your tongue on the roof of your mouth, sit for several minutes and allow the stored emotions within you to process through you. You don't need to know what they are about. Simply sit with your hands in the position described and allow your body to process. Your body stores many emotions, and you may never have access to what they are. But if you simply allow them to process through you, they can be released as is for your highest good. Stuck emotions equal poor mental and spiritual health or disease. Allowing the emotions to move equals health and vibrancy. Simply allow yourself to detox emotions at this time. You can set a timer or look at the clock and do this meditation for three to seven minutes. Just sit in quiet meditation with your hands in the suggested position, allowing your being to integrate and reshuffle the emotional decks within you.

8. After the time is completed, you may release your hands from the mudra and place them in your lap or at your sides, face up and palms open. Now, allow yourself to simply observe what you're feeling emotionally. Allow yourself to notice how you feel. You might feel sleepy or bored. You might feel sad or melancholy. You might feel happy or agitated. You might feel any number of other emotions. You might even be aware of fear underlying your other emotions. Just observe all of these feelings. None is good or bad. They just exist. They're just energy. They are impermanent, ever-moving, fluid energies. You can watch them and even direct them, but they're not you. You are the witness who sits and simply watches the inner show. Allow yourself to mindfully observe your emotions. Sometimes you can let the part of yourself that is like a wise mother or father participate. That's the part that might tell you ways to calm and quiet your emotions and care for yourself in a more loving manner. Even that is simply an aspect of you to be witnessed by the one who is behind it all, who is ever neutral, and ever at peace. This is your true self.

WATCHING THE BREATH

Meditation can be a state of being. The state of meditation manifests when we can become completely and mindfully present. In meditation, we accept the present moment for what it is and through this acceptance, we are living within the present moment wholly and completely. When in a state of meditation, we no longer travel into the future or past with our mind. We become totally present and mindfully grounded in the "now." The most compelling tool that can be used to accomplish this is our breathing. When we focus our attention to intentionally watch or follow the breath, we are able to come back to the present moment. We can use the breath to anchor our mind to the very moment when we are taking the breath. The breath is a direct pathway from the mind to the body and allows our whole being to come into the present moment. Creating awareness of the breath not only assists with achieving a meditative state, but it also helps us become more mindful in our everyday life. We breathe many times a day and are often unconscious of this process. Unconscious breaths are usually shallow and superficial, only filling and emptying the lungs partially. It is more common to see people breathing this way, using only their chest to breathe. This type of breath does not allow proper release of stale air and toxins from the inner recesses of the lungs. This is why learning to breathe fully, properly, and consciously can vastly improve our health.

We start by first considering the way we are breathing. More often than not, people flatten the belly and breathe rapidly only into the chest. The very best thing you can do is to first let go of the belly! Let the belly become big when you breathe, and release the abdominal muscles throughout your day. This simple step will allow you to breathe deeper and give our respiratory muscles a break. When the belly is working to be tightened and flexed, the weaker abdominal muscles have to work harder. To understand and visualize the ideal breath, look at a sleeping baby. The baby breathes deeply—into the belly first. A baby's whole body will expand with the complete breath. We want to return to the way we breathed as babies. As we grew and our minds began to impact our physical processes and we experienced traumatic or emotional states, our breathing changed. We can begin changing the breathing back by first observing the breaths that we are taking.

The easiest way to do this is by finding a comfortable position lying on your back or seated, if that is more comfortable. You can use your attention to notice where the breath is going naturally and then gently release the belly if it is flexed. You are working toward a state of meditation by "watching the breath." A great way to discover how you are breathing and when your breathing changes is by analyzing its depth and quality at different times throughout the day, especially when your mood or state of mind changes. There are many benefits to using breathing techniques such as these. You can learn to change your mood and physical state by bringing your attention to your breath. It is the simplest and most accessible tool available and allows increased focus and stress reduction. The breath can energize you when you are feeling drained. You can reduce anxiety, enhance sleeping patterns, and detox the body using deep, conscious breathing.

Using the "watching the breath" meditation tool brings important self-reflection and insight about our daily life. Noticing how the breath changes throughout the day and throughout life gives insight into emotions and thoughts. Some experiences or processes seem to cause us to hold our breath, which can contribute to the higher level of stress we may feel at certain times. We can learn to check in with the breath more often to revolutionize how we relate to ourselves and our bodies. We can become more present with ourselves by being aware of the breath. Very quickly we may find that this practice creates tranquility within the mind and allows the brain to work more efficiently. The mind can actually perpetuate a state of stress and anxiety as it feeds a loop of thoughts. These could be thoughts that are assisting in the release of a flow of stress hormones such as cortisol. Many immune diseases are linked to an overactive stress response. Allowing attention to come to the breath can quiet the mind in a way that actually allows the mind and body to relax, which can reduce the risk of disease. Many studies assert the physical benefits of meditation on the brain and body, and even more that have found the mental benefits of quieting the mind. The stillness we find may even allow us to make decisions more easily. We may be able to release physical tension we are storing. The body and mind are an interwoven circuit, and the breath is the life force that connects it all. Without conscious breathing, we become disconnected from ourselves.

Watching the Breath Meditation

Set up your environment by finding a quiet and comfortable place. You may light a candle, incense, or anything else that may help you to create a relaxed atmosphere. Choose a duration of time you would like to practice this meditation and set a timer. Try to start with at least three to five minutes. Commit yourself to this amount of time and allow your mind to let go of tracking time. Find a suitable position—lying on your back, sitting cross-legged, or sitting in a chair with both of your feet flat on the floor.

1. Gently exhale through your nose, completely emptying all breath from the lungs. Allow the breath to flow through your nose and into the lungs naturally, without changing anything in any way. As the breath flows in, follow it with your awareness. Notice the breath as it flows into the nostrils and down into the lungs. Notice the body expand. As you exhale, notice the breath as it leaves the body. Notice the body empty and collapse.

2. On your next inhalation, relax and exaggerate the belly. Allow the belly to expand and fill up like a big balloon. As you exhale, let the belly button fall toward the spine and allow the belly to empty completely. Begin to create a three-part full yogic breath. Do this by first filling the belly, then moving the breath upward to fill the rib cage, and finally allowing the chest to expand as it fills with air. Inhale deeply using this three-part full yogic breath.

3. Exhale completely in the reverse order. First empty the chest, then the rib cage, and then the belly. Continue these three-part full yogic breaths while keeping your attention on the sensations associated with each breath. Allow yourself to just be. This is a time to allow yourself to sit with what is. You are not striving for anything. Your only task is to breathe with awareness.

4. Use each breath as an opportunity to anchor your mind back into the present. It may help to use words to focus on. For example, as you inhale you may say silently in your mind, "I am breathing in," and as you exhale, "I am breathing out."

5. It may also help to find a location in the body to focus your awareness with each breath. You may choose your third eye, or *Ajna* (between your eyebrows) chakra, if you are feeling more intellectual. You may choose your heart center, or *Anahata* (center of your chest) chakra, if you are feeling more emotional. Use this point of awareness to anchor your breath as you visualize your breath leaving the body and returning into it at his location. Each time you notice your mind wander, bring your awareness back by noticing each inhalation and exhalation.

6. After your timer has gone off, notice any new sensations. Do you feel a sense of tranquility or stillness? Do thoughts seem more focused? These are some of the many benefits you may find after this meditation.

OBSERVING YOUR THOUGHTS

Using your awareness to watch the mind is another tool that can be used to reach a deeper meditative state. Sometimes this type of meditation is referred to as insight meditation. It can often be the next step in watching the breath. After you have calmed the mind to focus on the breath, you can continue to notice the thoughts that come. It is believed, particularly by Buddhists, that this deep type of insight meditation is the path to enlightenment. The trick to this process is a non-judgmental attitude. We do not judge ourselves for having thoughts. We do not attach ourselves or our identity to the thoughts. We create a separation between the mind and the observer. The true self is not the mind, neither is it the body. The true self is the observer. The true self is the silent witness of the mind. The true self is stillness. Its form is omnipresent light. It is believed that through this meditation, the Buddha achieved enlightenment. Without aiming for this outcome, we can still receive many benefits from this practice. We can experience improved health by reducing levels of stress and anxiety and, ultimately, have more restful sleep. We can begin to notice the inner processes of the mind, allowing us to follow our thoughts and notice how thoughts can become a chain reaction when we do not have intentional mindfulness. We can slow those thoughts down, reducing the mental chatter and creating a quiet mind. Many people notice that they become more connected to other people through compassion, more connected to the living world around them, and more connected to their true selves. Many experience reduction of symptoms of mood disorders such as anxiety and depression when they are able to watch their mind nonjudgmentally. You use this meditation to practice non-attachment, which can extend to your daily life in so many ways. It can reduce your emotional reactivity and enhance your ability to carefully think before you act and speak.

Watching the Mind Meditation

Prepare your environment by finding a quiet and comfortable place. Include anything that may help to set a relaxed atmosphere. Choose a time you would like to practice meditation and set a timer to allow yourself to let go of mentally tracking time. Try to start with five to ten minutes. Find a comfortable position. This begins in a similar manner to "Watching the Breath Meditation."

1. Bring your awareness first to your breath. Breathing through your nose, exhale all the breath from your lungs and then naturally allow the breath to flow into your lungs through your nose. As the breath flows in, follow it with your awareness.

2. As you inhale, begin to exaggerate the belly, allowing it to expand and fill up like a big balloon. As you exhale, let the navel fall toward the spine and allow the belly to empty while exhaling completely. Begin the three-part full yogic breath.

3. Now allow yourself to just be with what is. This is a time to allow yourself to sit in the moment as it comes. Your only task is to breathe and be. Begin to notice your mind. If your mind is very busy, you may use thoughts to anchor yourself to the breath. As you inhale you could tell yourself silently, "I am not this body," and as you exhale, "I am not this mind." This reminds you that you are not the body or the mind. You are the silent witness. You are the observer of the mind and of the breath.

4. Notice when thoughts come into the mind. Thoughts will come, and that is okay. As thoughts come, try not to fight or resist them. Try to practice non-judgment of the thoughts. Each time you notice a thought, do just that—notice it.

5. Notice your thoughts as a continuous flow, as if you are noticing waves crashing in from the ocean or clouds floating through the sky. Notice the thought, and notice it go as you allow the thoughts to pass by. Notice the next thought, and notice it pass. Notice yourself noticing the thoughts as they pass. Keep noticing your breath as each breath comes.

6. Remember that thoughts are okay. They will come, so try not to judge the thoughts and feelings, especially the ones you have about the fact that you are having thoughts. Notice yourself judging yourself. Notice yourself noticing yourself. Stay with the three-part full yogic breaths. Use each breath as an opportunity to fasten your mind back into the present. Use the words that focus on inhaling and exhaling if you find your mind is wandering quickly. Notice the wandering mind and come back to the breath.

7. You are not resisting thoughts. You are observing them. You are allowing them to float by. You are curious about them but not attached to them. They do not control you. You are not your mind. Notice the stillness that may arrive. Notice the space between the thoughts. Continue noticing as long as possible or until the timer goes off. Allow yourself to come back very slowly and gently after your timer goes off. Practice this meditation daily, and use this practice as a part of your daily life.

8. Always remember: You are not your body or your mind. You are a silent witness. We can begin to deepen this understanding by using the power of the breath. We can watch ourselves breathe and observe the body. This helps us understand that we are separate from the body. We are watching the body. Watching the mind allows us to gain insight and go even deeper, understanding that we are not only our thoughts but we are also infinite and witnessing our existence while simultaneously living it. We are watching the mind. These two processes can help us achieve meditation. You may find you are meditating and suddenly you have the thought, *Hey, I am meditating*! which effectively ends your blissful state of meditation. This is okay. Come back and keep observing. The space that you feel between the thoughts and breaths is meditation. The serenity and bliss you feel between the thoughts show that you have achieved that state of meditation that allows you to feel your true essence.

MINDFUL RELATIONSHIPS

The purpose of practicing mindfulness is not just to achieve a feeling of calmness. It is to improve your quality of life. When you're able to cultivate a more mindful approach to your day, you are able to be fully present in whatever you're doing. When you're able to be completely present, you're often drastically more effective, whether you're trying to accomplish a task, interact with somebody, or generate a new idea. Complete and utter presence and mindfulness may be the keys to peak performance.

In the dance of intimacy, the concept of bringing mindfulness into relationships is a valuable one to consider. If you're able to bring mindfulness, for example, to your romantic relationships, imagine how they might be different. What if you were able to be 100 percent present with your partner and yourself during any given exchange of love, caring, passion, or even conflict?

How many times during a disagreement with a significant other are you thinking ahead to what you're going to say next instead of being mindful and listening to what your partner is trying to express? It is part of human nature to try to defend when we're feeling attacked. It's also human nature to lash out or exhibit certain behaviors when we feel threatened either physically or emotionally. When we have a disagreement with somebody we care about, we often feel less safe. We feel like a piece of our emotional health might be impacted because of the dissension.

Throw our neurotic inner voice into the mix during any given exchange, and we have a whole chaotic narrative in our own minds. Then we miss the opportunity to be present and listen to our partner. You can see how being mindful during times of strife in a relationship could be valuable. In those cases, we would be more available to validate our partner's feelings and come to mutual agreement about troublesome issues.

What about during the good times or just the neutral times? How many peak experiences have we missed the full depth and scope of because we were distracted by our mind's urge to multitask? Imagine you're parasailing with your partner. You're attached to parachutes floating high above the ocean. Below you there sits a sparkling sea with sunlight glinting off its surface and green turtles swimming in the waves. It's easy to be more present in that moment because it's novel. But if it's not a peak experience, are you ever 100 percent present and mindful in the moment? How frequently? Take an inventory of how present you're able to stay in your relationships—and not just in romantic relationships. Think about the last conversation you had with a friend. How frequently did your mind wander?

Nowadays, the ultimate enemy of mindfulness is a smartphone. How many times do you see people having dinner together and at least one person is on the phone, looking utterly engaged in whatever they're texting or doing. This is at the expense of presence with the other people. And there's no judgment here because we've all done it. And we will all probably do it again. But when we bring awareness to our level of mindfulness, we have an opportunity to make a conscious choice if we would like to work to change it. Practicing mindfulness and meditation on a regular basis gives us access to more ability to be present. And then it is our choice if we want to tap into that skill.

Mindful Relationships Meditation

You can use this meditation to increase your ability to stay present and be mindful during relationship-based interactions. It is like weight lifting for your mind and heart.

In a relationship, any interaction is really one of the heart. Whether you define the heart as the organ that pumps your blood, the emotional energy center in the center of your chest, or the complicated chemical symphony coursing through your body, love is truly at the center of the matter.

In this meditation, we will embrace the heart and invite it to feel emotionally safe and nurtured. When the heart feels safe, we lessen the likelihood of distractions of an emotional nature that may take us outside of our focused presence. In Greek mythology, the goddess Aphrodite was known to govern love, pleasure, relationships, matters of the heart, and romantic unions. We will invite her archetype to school us in how to have mindful, harmonious, joyous relationships of all kinds.

Find a comfortable place for this meditation. Make sure you will be undisturbed for fifteen to thirty minutes. This is a wonderful meditation to do lying down, if you are able. You really want to allow yourself to relax deeply during this process.

1. Spend a few minutes noticing your breath as it comes in and goes out of your mouth or nose. Feel the sensation of air moving and passing through those areas of your body. Notice how it feels as it goes deeper into your lungs and how it feels as you blow it out as slowly as you can. Bring your focus to that air and really try to fill your lungs like two balloons. What if you could fully inflate them? What might that feel like? Bring the breath deeply into the base of your lungs all the way down. When you exhale, feel your lung tissue being revitalized. Feel the fresh air you're bringing in oxygenate your body and feel the carbon dioxide and other components of the air you blow out. Feel yourself letting go of that which you no longer need.

2. In Chinese medicine, your lungs are oftentimes the storehouse for grief energy. Deep breathing is one of the most effective ways to gently and easily let go of deep-seated grief. We all have grief in our heart and our lungs. Whether for specific life events or, more frequently, for things in our world or the world around us, it's a natural part of being human. But if we can mitigate that grief energy, help it to flow, and let it go just as easily as it was acquired, we give ourselves the opportunity to have a more open heart and to feel greater levels of emotional freedom.

3. Use the power of deep breathing even as you're walking to work or grabbing groceries at the supermarket. Do some deep breathing and oxygenate and cleanse your physical lungs as well as your lungs' emotional energy. Let the emotional energy that no longer needs to be stored be released easily and gently through breathing.

5. Relationships are a dance of energy and light steeped down to physical, nonphysical, verbal, emotional, and mental interactions of every kind. But in the most basic sense, any interaction with another person, animal, or plant is an exchange of energy.

6. So, as you feel yourself in this restful meditative place, contemplate, without judgment, the interactions that you have with other people. Specifically, focus on the romantic interactions. Allow yourself to see, feel, and know which interactions and energy exchanges enhance you, which are neutral, and which deplete you. Simply notice this information. There is no pressure now to take action on it. It simply exists.

7. Now invite the benevolent, life-affirming presence of the archetypal goddess Aphrodite into your meditation by stating the following internally or aloud, "I ask that all that transpires in this meditation be for the very highest good of all life and in accordance with universal natural law, helping all and harming none. I ask that the goddess Aphrodite infuse the room and space in which I am meditating right now with her loving, ecstatic light. I now decree that my relationships will be harmonious, fulfilling, joyful, and full of infinite, unconditional love. I commit to being present in my relationships. I invite my relationship partners to do the same with great love and care. It is done."

8. Remember that love is free. It transcends space and time. It does not require physical proximity. Love is an ever-flowing energy and yet it is also tangible and intangible, imaginative and real, particles and waves. Love is an infinite paradox because it is all things. We live in a paradoxical universe, and love is the energy that powers it.

9. Contemplate the infinite nature of love as you use the word *love* like a mantra. Simply repeat it internally as you meditate. Whenever your mind wanders simply say the word *love*. Allow yourself to notice each time you say the word *love* what it evokes. What do you feel? Do you envision a certain color? Or picture? Do you think of a certain person? Do you hear a song or sound in your mind when you say the word *love* within yourself? Do you smell fragrant roses or blooming jasmine? What is love for you on a sensory level? Let this awareness bubble up with no effort on your part. Allow yourself to rest in an infinite ocean of love. Float on its surface in complete relaxation and surrender to the infinite reality that is the truth of existence. You are love.

10. When you are ready, bring your attention back into your body and into the room. Feel yourself present in this reality. Use your hands to rub your feet, legs, arms, and shoulders and say aloud, "I am here now. I am present." Make sure you drink plenty of water. It is important to be well hydrated after you meditate because your body may be engaging in self-healing as a result, and proper hydration can aid in the process.

11. The essence of infinite love with which you connected will help you feel a greater level of internal safety. And the intention to be present and mindful in your relationships will gently permeate your life.

MINDFUL DHARMA

In Buddhist philosophy, the concept of dharma is all about your life's purpose. It's the essence of the service that you share with the world and humanity. We all have a dharma or life purpose. Sometimes it's easy to see what that is. There are some people who you can see living their dharma through their career. But others have dharmic fulfillment through different areas of their life. Nothings better or worse, it all just exists.

The truth of your dharma rests in the fact that you matter. Your existence matters. And every single person has a unique, special, meaningful purpose for existence—whether that purpose is easy to spot or subtle.

Cultivating mindfulness and being able to rest in the spaces between your thoughts can help you connect with your dharma. When you are meditating, you are aligning with your dharma. And even by living a mindful life you are harmonizing with your life's purpose. When you bring full presence into your existence the important parts of it come into greater focus with more ease.

In the following meditation, designed to bring mindfulness to your life and its purpose, we will connect with the archetypal deity known as Shiva, Hindu figurehead of the divine masculine. Shiva is known for his beautiful dance of light, bringing things into being. He displays divine leadership qualities and offers these talents and more to you for integration into your dharma and your soul's purpose.

Mindful Dharma Meditation

1. Get comfortable and take a few minutes to quiet your mind. Follow your breath and observe your thoughts as you slow down your brain waves by meditating. Take a few minutes and use the process of inhaling and exhaling to bring yourself into a mindful, meditative state.

2. In this meditation, we use an ancient mantra that is popular to this day. It provides a connection to the Hindu deity known as Shiva. Repeat the following mantra in your mind for several minutes, "*Om na ma Shiva.*" This means, "I connect to my inner self with the help of the being Shiva."

3. Rest in the spaces between the syllables of the words contained in the mantra. Allow your brainwave patterns to alter as you sink more deeply into the sound of this mantra. Continue repeating it and allow yourself to envision a radiant turquoise blue in your mind's eye. See this refracted wave of light before you and watch it expand into a nebula of bright turquoise.

4. Feel your consciousness being drawn into this turquoise nebula. No effort is required. You will just naturally merge with it. As that happens, continue repeating the mantra and feel this radiant turquoise light begin to infuse your body. This light is from Lord Shiva—a gift of the essence of radiance. As it integrates with your body and your cells, it's like a key in a lock unlocking any doors that separate you from your divine purpose.

5. You are now aligned with your dharma. Repeat the following internally or aloud, "I am now fully aligned with my soul's highest purpose for my highest good. I live my dharma with joy and ease, and I am prosperous, vivacious, and healthy. My life is filled with harmony and fulfillment. It is done."

6. Now, continue to rest in that turquoise light. Repeat the mantra as you do this, and feel your consciousness slowly sliding back within your being. Feel it begin to rest behind your being. Relax your shoulders. Think back into your witnessing self. Witness yourself repeating the mantra. Witness the radiant turquoise light you experienced. Witness it all. Allow your internal witness to easily see your soul's highest progress. Your inner witness will feel detached from it but will lovingly support you as you live it to its fullest. Rest in this state for as long as you'd like. When you're ready, bring your awareness back into the room, connect with your ability to be mindful by noticing the sights, sounds, and smells you're experiencing. You can tell yourself, "I am here now," as you use your hands to vigorously pat or rub your arms, legs, and feet and make sure you're fully present in your body before you continue with your day.

conclusion

I hope you have enjoyed your journey into mindfulness! As you've learned in this book, living a mindful life is an art and a science. There's not necessarily a step-by-step process that works for everyone but instead a wide variety of beautiful and useful techniques that you can sample to determine what will help you create a life of meaning and presence. For many thousands of years, human beings have endeavored to be mindful. Now it's your turn to find what works for you. As you live each day present in the moments and mindfully experiencing your life, may you experience joy, harmony, and happiness. May your life be filled with love!

ACKNOWLEDGMENTS

I would like to thank the talented team at Sterling Ethos. Kate Zimmermann is everything an author could ask for in an editor. I feel truly grateful to get to work with her again. She is a consummate professional and a joy. Ashten Luna has done a beautiful job helping midwife this book into being. I'd also like to thank the talented copy editor Kate Matracia at NounSense LLC, project editor Hannah Reich, and designers who made this book look so beautiful and flow so smoothly.

I am incredibly lucky to be graced with the presence of an exemplary literary agent and person. Lisa Hagan has become like family and has made my dreams come true again and again. I send infinite gratitude to her for all of her amazing work.

Dr. Laurie Nadel listened to spirit, made the necessary connections possible, and enabled my career as an author, and I'm eternally grateful. Mary Lively Jamison spent many hours in the trenches teaching me the ins and outs of technical, nonfiction writing back before I had an agent or platform. Her lessons rubbed off on me and I am tremendously grateful!

I feel incredibly fortunate to be surrounded by an amazing support system of family, friends, and colleagues. There are too many of you to name, but you're all amazing and you keep me afloat as I navigate the sea of creativity and business. A few standout soul sisters include Jamie Eslinger—my twinsie and marketing maven extraordinaire, Shannon Kaiser—a super-soulful author teammate spreading love far and wide, and Emma Mildon—a shining light of positivity. Together we rise and share the love.

ABOUT THE AUTHOR

Amy Leigh Mercree's motto is "Live joy. Be kind. Love unconditionally." She counsels women and men in the underrated art of self-love to create happier lives. Amy is a bestselling author, media personality, and medical intuitive. Mercree speaks internationally focusing on kindness, joy, and wellness.

Mercree is the bestselling author of *The Spiritual Girl's Guide to Dating: Your Enlightened Path to Love, Sex, and Soul Mates, A Little Bit of Chakras: An Introduction to Energy Healing, Joyful Living: 101 Ways to Transform Your Spirit and Revitalize Your Life, The Chakras and Crystals Cookbook: Juices, Sorbets, Smoothies, Salads, and Crystal Infusions to Empower Your Energy Centers, The Compassion Revolution: 30 Days of Living from the Heart, A Little Bit of Meditation: An Introduction to Being Present, Essential Oils Handbook: Recipes for Natural Living, Apple Cider Vinegar Handbook: Recipes for Natural Living,* and *The Mood Book: Crystals, Mantras, and Rituals to Elevate Your Spirit.*

Mercree has been featured in *Glamour, Women's Health, Inc., Soul & Spirit,* and *Shape* magazines, *The Huffington Post,* Your Tango and Mind Body Green websites, CBS, NBC, and many more.

Check out AmyLeighMercree.com for articles, powerful quotes, and quizzes. Mercree is fast becoming one of the most quoted women on the Web. See what all the buzz is about @AmyLeighMercree on Twitter, Snapchat, and Instagram.

To download your FREE mindfulness toolkit
and calm your hectic brain right now, go to
www.amyleighmercree.com/mindfulnesstoolkit.
The password is MINDNFULNESS.

REFERENCES

INTRODUCTION

"4 Celebrity Quotes on Meditation." mindbodygreen. March 21, 2011. Accessed February 08, 2018. https://www.mindbodygreen.com/0-2151/4-Celebrity-Quotes-on-Meditation.html.

"7 Celebrity Quotes On Mindfulness." Soul and Spirit. November 7, 2017. Accessed February 08, 2018. http://www.soulandspiritmagazine. com/7-celebrity-quotes-mindfulness/.

"33 Famous People You Didn't Know Practice Meditation." Feeling Success. November 8, 2015. Accessed February 8, 2018. https://www. feelingsuccess.com/famous-people-who-meditate/.

Center for Mindfulness. "History of MBSR." University of Massachusetts Medical School. November 17, 2016. Accessed February 8, 2018. http: //feelingsuccess.com/?p=5693.

"Getting Started with Mindfulness." Mindful. January 19, 2018. Accessed February 08, 2018. https://www.mindful.org/meditation/ mindfulness-getting-started/.

Santilli, Elyse. "10 Easy Ways You Can Practice Mindfulness." *The Huffington Post*. September 2, 2015. Accessed February 8, 2018. https://www. huffingtonpost.com/elyse-gorman/10-easy-ways-you-can-practice-mindfulness_b_8069422.html.

Thompson, Alexandra. "Mindfulness championed by Gwyneth Paltrow and Emma Watson reduces stress levels by MORE THAN half by changing the brain's structure." *Daily Mail*. October 12, 2017. Accessed February 8, 2018. http://www.dailymail.co.uk/health/article-4948608/Mindfulness-championed-Gwyneth-Paltrow-reduces-stress.html.

"What Celebrities Say About Meditation." Celebrity Meditation Quotes: Learn How Meditation Changed Their Lives | Breethe Meditation App. 2016. Accessed February 8, 2018. https://breethe.com/ celebrities-and-meditation-quotes/.

THE HISTORY OF MINDFULNESS

"History of Mindfulness: From East to West and From Religion to Science."
Positive Psychology Program. March 13, 2017.

Shea, Christopher. "A Brief History of Mindfulness in the USA and Its Impact
on Our Lives." PsychCentral. 2016. https://psychcentral.com/lib/a-brief-
history-of-mindfulness-in-the-usa-and-its-impact-on-our-lives/.

Bushak, Lecia. "A Brief History of Yoga: From Ancient Hindu Scriptures
to The Modern, Westernized Practice." *Medical Daily*. October 21,
2015. https://www.medicaldaily.com/brief-history-yoga-ancient-hindu-
scriptures-modern-westernized-practice-358162.

"Jon Kabat-Zinn." Wikipedia. 2018. https://en.wikipedia.org/wiki/
Jon_Kabat-Zinn.

"Mindfulness-Based Cognitive Therapy." *Psychology Today*. 2018.
Sussex Publishers. www.psychologytoday.com/us/therapy-types/
mindfulness-based-cognitive-therapy.

"Sammasati: An Exposition of Right Mindfulness." Ven. P. A. Payutto.
2018. http://www.abuddhistlibrary.com/Buddhism/B%20-%20
Theravada/Teachers/Ven%20Payutto/Sammasati/Sammasati%20An%20
Exposition%20of%20Right%20Mindfulness.htm.

Rosenbaum, Robert, and Barry Magid. What's Wrong with Mindfulness (and
What Isn't): Zen Perspectives. Wisdom, 2016.

THE SCIENCE OF MINDFULNESS

Mindful Staff. "Jon Kabat-Zinn: Defining Mindfulness." *Mindful*. April
4, 2017. Accessed February 2, 2018. https://www.mindful.org/
jon-kabat-zinn-defining-mindfulness/.

"Center for Mindfulness—UMass Medical School." University of
Massachusetts Medical School. June 24, 2014. Accessed February 2, 2018.
https://www.umassmed.edu/cfm/.

"The Jha Lab." The Jha Lab RSS. Accessed February 2, 2018. http://www.
amishi.com/lab/military/.

Chambers, Richard, Barbara Chuen Yee Lo, and Nicholas B. Allen. "The Impact of Intensive Mindfulness Training on Attentional Control, Cognitive Style, and Affect." *Cognitive Therapy and Research* 32, no. 3, 2007: 303–22. https://link.springer.com/article/10.1007/s10608-007-9119-0.

Hofmann, S., A. Sawyer, A. Witt, and D. Oh. "The effect of mindfulness-based therapy on anxiety and depression: A meta-analytic review". *Journal of Consulting and Clinical Psychology*, 78(2), 2010: 169–183. http://dx.DOI.org/10.1037/a0018555.

Goyal M., S. Singh, E. Sibinga, et al. "Meditation Programs for Psychological Stress and Well-being: A Systematic Review and Meta-analysis." *JAMA Internal Medicine*, 174(3): 2014: 357–368. https://jamanetwork.com/journals/jamainternalmedicine/fullarticle/1809754.

Farb N., A. Anderson, H. Mayberg, J. Bean, D. McKeon, Z. V. Segal. "Minding One's Emotions: Mindfulness Training Alters the Neural Expression of Sadness." *Emotion*, 10(1). 2010: 25–33. https://www.ncbi.nim.nih.gov/pmc/articles/PMC501/7873/.

Ortner, C. N. M., S. Kilner, and P. Zelazo. "Mindfulness meditation and reduced emotional interference on a cognitive task." *Motivation and Emotion*. (2007) 31: 271. https://DOI.org/10.1007/s11031-007-9076-7

Tan, Lucy B. G., Barbara C. Y. Lo, and C. Neil Macrae. "Brief Mindfulness Meditation Improves Mental State Attribution and Empathizing." *PLoS ONE*. 2014:9(10): e110510. https://DOI.org/10.1371/journal.pone.0110510.

Black, D. S., and G. M. Slavich. "Mindfulness Meditation and the Immune System: A Systematic Review of Randomized Controlled Trials." *Annals of the New York Academy of Sciences*. 1373(1). 2016:13–24. DOI: 10.1111/nyas.12998.

Wachs, K. and J. Cordova. "Mindful relating: exploring mindfulness and emotion repertoires in intimate relationships." *Journal of Marital and Family Therapy*. 33(4). 2007: 464–481. DOI: 10.1111/j.1752-0606.2007.00032.x.

Hutcherson, Cendri A., Emma M. Seppala, and James J. Gross. "Loving-Kindness Meditation Increases Social Connectedness." *Emotion*. 8(5). 2008: 720–724. http://dx.DOI.org/10.1037/a0013237

Jha, Amishi P., Elizabeth A. Stanley, Anastasia Kiyonaga, Ling Wong, and Lois Gelfand. "Examining the Protective Effects of Mindfulness Training on Working Memory Capacity and Affective Experience." *Emotion*. 10(1). 2010: 54–64. http://dx.DOI.org/10.1037/a0018438.

Moore, A., and P. Malinowski. "Meditation, Mindfulness and Cognitive Flexibility." *Conscious Cognition*. 18(1). 2009: 176–86. https://www.ncbi.nlm.nih.gov/pubmed/19181542.

Hofmann, Stefan G., et al. Advances in Pediatrics., U.S. National Library of Medicine, Apr. 2010, www.ncbi.nlm.nih.gov/pmc/articles/PMC2848393/.

Black, D. S., and G. M. Slavich. "Mindfulness Meditation and the Immune System: A Systematic Review of Randomized Controlled Trials." *Annals of the New York Academy of Sciences*. 1373(1). 2016:13–24. DOI: 10.1111/nyas.12998.

Tan L. B. G., B. C. Y. Lo, and C. N. Macrae. Brief Mindfulness Meditation Improves Mental State Attribution and Empathizing. PLoS ONE. 2014. 9(10): e110510. https://DOI.org/10.1371/journal.pone.0110510.

Wachs, K. & J. Cordova. Mindful relating: exploring mindfulness and emotion repertoires in intimate relationships. *Journal of Marital and Family Therapy*. 33(4). 2007. 464-481. DOI: 10.1111/j.1752-0606.2007.00032.x.

Wachs, K. & J. Cordova. Mindful relating: exploring mindfulness and emotion repertoires in intimate relationships. *Journal of Marital and Family Therapy*. 33(4). 2007. 464-481. DOI: 10.1111/j.1752-0606.2007.00032.x.

QUIETING THE CHEMICAL SYMPHONY

Brand, Serge, Edith Holsboer-Trachsler, José Raúl Naranjo, and Stefan Schmidt. "Influence of Mindfulness Practice on Cortisol and Sleep in Long-Term and Short-Term Meditators." *Neuropsychobiology*. 65, 2012:109–118. DOI: 10.1159/000330362.

Espel, E. S., E. Puterman, J. Lin, E. H. Blackburn, P. Y. Lum, N. D. Beckmann, J. Zhu, E. Lee, A. Gilbert, R. A. Rissman, R. E. Tanzi, and E.E. Schadt. "Meditation and Vacation Effects Have an Impact on Disease-Associated Molecular Phenotypes." *Translational Psychiatry*. 6, e88 (2016): 164. DOI: 10.1038/tp.2016.164.

Fjorback, Lone Overby. "Mindfulness and Bodily Distress." *Danish Medical Journal*. 59, 11 (2012): 1–18.

O'Leary, Karen, Siobhan O'Neill, Samantha Dockray. "A Systematic Review of the Effects of Mindfulness Interventions on Cortisol." *Journal of Health Psychology*. 21, 9 (2015): 2108–2121. DOI: 10.1177/1359105315569095.

Staff, *Mindful*. "Jon Kabat-Zinn: Defining Mindfulness." *Mindful*. April 4, 2017. Accessed February 2, 2018. https://www.mindful.org/jon-kabat-zinn-defining-mindfulness/.

"Center for Mindfulness - UMass Medical School." University of Massachusetts Medical School. June 24, 2014. Accessed February 02, 2018. https://www.umassmed.edu/cfm/.

Chambers, Richard, Barbara Chuen Yee Lo, and Nicholas B. Allen. "The Impact of Intensive Mindfulness Training on Attentional Control, Cognitive Style, and Affect." *Cognitive Therapy and Research* 32, no. 3, 2007: 303-22. DOI: 10.1007/s10608-007-9119-0.

Hofmann, S., A. Sawyer, A. Witt, and D. Oh. "The effect of mindfulness-based therapy on anxiety and depression: A meta-analytic review". *Journal of Consulting and Clinical Psychology*, 78(2), 2010. 169-183. http://dx.DOI.org/10.1037/a0018555.

MINDFULNESS AND THE BRAIN

Chen, Fangfang; Lv, Xueyu; Fang, Jiliang; Yu, Shan; Sui, Jing; Fan, Lingzhong; Li, Tao; Hong, Yang; Wang, XiaoLing; Wang, Weidong; Jiang, Tianzi "The Effect of Body-Mind Relaxation Meditation Induction on Major Depressive Disorder: A Resting-State fMRI Study. *Journal of Affective Disorders*. 183, (2015): 75–82. DOI: 10.1016/j.jad.2015.04.030.

Chopra, Deepak. "Why Meditate?" DeepakChopra.com. March. 2017. Accessed: February 2018. https://www.deepakchopra.com/blog/article/4701.

Davidson, Richard J. "Affective Style, Psychopathology, and Resilience: Brain Mechanisms and Plasticity." *American Psychology.* 55 (2000); 1196–1214.

Davidson, Richard J., Jon Kabat-Zinn, Jessica Schumacher, Melissa Rosenkranz, Daniel Muller, Saki F. Santorelli, Ferris Urbanowski, Anne Harrington, Katherine Bonus, and John Sheridan. "Alterations in Brain and Immune Function Produced by Mindfulness Meditation." *Psychosomatic Medicine* 65 no. 4. (July 2003): 564–570. DOI: 10.1097/01.PSY.0000077505.67574.E3.

Fletcher, Lindsay. Benjamin Schoendorff, and Steven Hayes. "Searching for Mindfulness in the Brain: A Process-Oriented Approach to Examining the Neural Correlates of Mindfulness." *Mindfulness* 1 (2010): 41–63. DOI: 10.1007/s12671-010-0006-5.

Young, Simon N. "Biologic Effects of Mindfulness Meditation: Growing Insights into Neurobiologic Aspects of the Prevention of Depression." *Journal of Psychiatry and Neuroscience* 36, 2 (2011): 75–77. DOI: 10.1503/jpn.110010.

TYPES OF MINDFULNESS PRACTICE

"22 Mindfulness Exercises, Techniques, and Activities for Adults." Positive Psychology Program, January 18, 2017.

Halse, Henry. "Tai Chi Basic Steps for Beginners." https://www.livestrong.com/article/431042-tai-chi-basic-steps-for-beginners/.

"Loving-Kindness Meditation." Greater Good in Action, 2018. https://ggia.berkeley.edu/practice/loving_kindness_meditation.

WATCHING THE INNER SHOW

Singer, Michael A. *The Untethered Soul: the Journey beyond Yourself.* New Harbinger Publications, Inc, 2008.

MINDFULNESS MEDITATIONS

"Raisin Meditation." Greater Good In Action: Science-based Practices for a Meaningful Life. University of California, Berkeley. Accessed February 28, 2018. https://ggia.berkeley.edu/practice/raisin_meditation#.

"Walking Meditation." Greater Good In Action: Science-based Practices for a Meaningful Life. University of California, Berkeley. Accessed February 28, 2018. https://ggia.berkeley.edu/practice/walking_meditation#data-tab-how.

Grossman, P., L. Niemann, S. Schmidt, and H. Walach. Mindfulness-based Stress Reduction and Health Benefits. A Meta-analysis. *Journal of Psychosomatic Research* 57(1) (July 2004): 95–109.

Siragusa, Nancy. "How to Eat Mindfully." *Good Food*. BBC. 2015. Accessed February 28, 2018. https://www.bbcgoodfood.com/howto/guide/how-eat-mindfully.

Willard, Christopher. "6 Ways to Practice Mindful Eating." Mindful.org. October 13, 2016. https://www.mindful.org/6-ways-practice-mindful-eating/.

Hussey, Rezzan. "The Remarkable Benefits of having Breath Awareness." Art of Well-Being. Accessed June 14, 2016. http://www.artofwellbeing.com/2016/06/14/breath-awareness/.

"Benefits of Mindful Breathing." Eco Institute, 2017. Accessed February 26, 2017. https://eocinstitute.org/meditation/meditation-and-breathing-benefits-of-mindful-breathing/.

"Vipassana Meditation Technique." Eco Institute, 2017. Accessed February 26, 2017. https://eocinstitute.org/meditation/vipassana-meditation-technique/.

INDEX